# 99

## of the best
# EXPERIENTIAL
# CORPORATE
# GAMES
## we know!

Simon Priest
Sam Sikes
Faith Evans

An eXperientia Publication

Printed in the United States of America
10  9  8  7  6  5  4  3  2  1

# Dedicated to **KARL ROHNKE**

**pioneer, entertainer, professional, and good friend.**

Karl has been a great "player" of games all his life. We owe him a debt of gratitude for influencing most of the games in this book.

# WAIVER

# INTRODUCTION from Simon

Subsequent to the publishing of last year's book: "101 of the best Corporate Teambuilding Activities we know," I suggested that 99 of the best games would be a good sequel. Sam and Faith agreed to collaborate and this book is the result. These games are experiential in design. This means that your key role as the facilitator is to add reflection, integration, and continuation elements to these activities.

This book's 99 games are placed into 6 categories and presented in a typical sequence that might be useful in most programs:

> 10 - WARMUPS get people's heart rates elevated or stretch
> their muscles and joints to avoid injuries;
> 17 - OPENERS set the program tone by detailing themes
> or introducing people to learn their names;
> 18 - SOCIALIZERS deinhibit people or familiarize them, so that
> they learn more than one another's names;
> 14 - FILLERS occupy unexpected program gaps with more,
> sedentary and time consuming games;
> 13 - ENERGIZERS quickly motivate, invigorate, or raise levels
> of enthusiasm through physical activity; and
> 27 - CLOSERS highlight learning, celebrate achievement, or
> bring new commitments for future change.

You can find a summary of the games on pages 212 and 213. You can find a breakdown of the games (by ideal duration, number of props, group size, and movement needed) on pages 214 and 215.

To give credit where credit is due, the origin of each activity is given as best we can discern and each one is also referenced to its original written form according to the following key:

| Number | CODE | Book (Author) |
|--------|------|---------------|
| 5 | EM | Executive Marbles (Sikes) |
| 1 | ZG | Zircon Gorilla (Sikes) |
| 6 | BBA | Bottomless Bag Again (Rohnke) |
| 5 | BPA | Back Pocket Adventure (Rohnke & Grout) |
| 2 | FSIV | Funn Stuff vol. IV (Rohnke) |

| 2 | FSIII | Funn Stuff vol. III (Rohnke) |
| 3 | FSII | Funn Stuff vol. II (Rohnke) |
| 2 | FSI | Funn Stuff vol. I (Rohnke) |
| 8 | QS | QuickSilver (Rohnke & Butler) |
| 11 | SB | Silver Bullets (Rohnke) |
| 2 | CC | Cowstails and Cobras (Rohnke) |
| 1 | NG | New Games (Fluegelman) |
| 1 | MNG | More New Games (Fluegelman) |
| 3 | PF | Playfair (Goodman & Weinstein) |
| 1 | UYN | 50 Ways to Use Your Noodle (Cavert & Sikes) |
| 46 | New | New ones (some with unknown attributions) |

99      Total Games (the best ones we know)

At this point, we'd like to thank Karl Rohnke and Project Adventure for their pioneer work cataloging and "keeping" the games that are a cornerstone to our professional work. If you like the games found here and would like to learn others, I recommend these books:

Sikes, S. (1998). Executive Marbles. Tulsa, OK: Learning Unlimited. (ISBN 0-9646541-2-1).

Sikes, S. (1995). Feeding the Zircon Gorilla. Tulsa, OK: Learning Unlimited. (ISBN 0-9646541-0-5).

Rohnke, K. (1991). The Bottomless Bag Again. Dubuque, IA: Kendall/Hunt. (ISBN 0-8403-8757-1).

Rohnke, K. & Grout, J. (1998). Back Pocket Adventure. Needham Heights, MA: Simon & Schuster and Project Adventure. (ISBN 0-536-01419-1).

Rohnke, K. (2000). Funn Stuff (vol. IV). Dubuque, IA: Kendall/Hunt. (ISBN 0-7872-7133-0).

Rohnke, K. (1998). Funn Stuff (vol. III). Dubuque, IA: Kendall/Hunt. (ISBN 0-7872-4654-9).

Rohnke, K. (1996). Funn Stuff (vol. II). Dubuque, IA: Kendall/Hunt. (ISBN 0-7872-2316-6).

Rohnke, K. (1996). Funn Stuff (vol. I). Dubuque, IA: Kendall/Hunt. (ISBN 0-7872-1633-X).

Rohnke, K. & Butler, S. (1995). QuickSilver. Dubuque, IA: Kendall/Hunt and Project Adventure. (ISBN 0-7872-0032-8).

Rohnke, K. (1984). Silver Bullets. Dubuque, IA: Kendall/Hunt and Project Adventure. (ISBN 0-8403-5682-X).

Rohnke, K. (1989). Cowstails and Cobras II. Dubuque, IA: Kendall/Hunt and Project Adventure. (ISBN 08403-5434-7).

# INTRODUCTION from Sam

GAMING SUCCESS:  Want to play?  Games for businesses and organizations can be some of the trickiest activities to facilitate. Imagine the common situation: This is the first time 30 people in a group have met you.  This activity must set the tone in ten minutes or less for what comes next.  You are responsible for transforming the new group from independent, random energy to a focused, structured unit.  It is possible!  The following paragraphs highlight some of the important factors to help ensure gaming success.

Choose a game with some forethought.  Make a conscious effort to match whatever game you facilitate with something related to the program or its expected outcomes.  Is there a physical component to the day?  Use a game that stretches muscles.  Will the day require people to be attentive?  Use an activity that requires people to listen and follow instructions.  Do you want people to learn to do things differently?  Use a game requiring creativity or non-linear thinking. If the activity has a clear purpose and this is mentioned, people will not feel silly playing the game...even if they look a little silly.

Use broad-based challenges.  Some people like puzzles, others like to socialize, still others like to get active and noisy.  If you will be doing several games, choose games that vary by how people like to participate.  Some people love tag games, but doing nothing but tag games will likely demotivate (and exhaust) others.  Facilitators tend to lead games they like to do.  Try ones that stretch your comfort.

Be confident.  No matter what happens, look and sound confident while giving instructions and while people are playing.  Participants who might not otherwise participate fully will join you, if what you lead looks, sounds, and smells like it is safe, fun, and worthwhile.

Maintain a positive attitude.  Project the attitude you want people to have.  If you want enthusiasm, you had better project enthusiasm. If you want people calm but engaged, project the same as you give instructions.  Use your voice and body movements to set the tone.

Move through the instructions.  Some facilitators have the gift I call "economy of words."  They say very little and yet folks understand exactly what they are supposed to do. Keep instructions as simple and direct as possible. If the instructions are given verbally, do not expect everyone to remember all the information and know what to do. People have an amazing capacity to learn from others as they proceed. Don't allow time for people to think about loopholes in an activity. Most activities are meant to be straightforward and fun.

<u>Demonstrate a quick example when possible</u>. Get physical with your instructions. If the group is supposed to shake hands and say a particular name, then you should show them what that interaction looks like and maybe have everyone practice it once for themselves.

<u>Move through the activity</u>. Once a game gets going, be aware of the group's energy or fun levels. Stop the game and go to the next one, before the group's momentum or its levels of energy and fun drop.

<u>Use participants as their own referees</u>. You cannot watch everyone all the time. Don't get caught up by playing the law enforcer for all players. Give the instructions and let people monitor themselves.

<u>Expect some chaos</u>. In my mind, I see activities going so smoothly and everyone doing what I expect they are supposed to do. Then reality sets in and I realize there will be some confusion because of differing perceptions, perspectives, history, and listening skills. Interactions may be chaotic for a moment, but people can adapt and standardize situations without your help, if you give them a chance.

<u>Learn from experience</u>. Experience means you can quickly recognize and capitalize on the unexpected. Experience does not mean you will know exactly how an activity will turn out. Is it safe? Is it fun? Is it reasonable? Is it legal, moral, ethical? People will take the initiative to change what you establish. Experience will allow you to make a judgment call whether to stop, discourage, or encourage what they do or change in an activity.

<u>Participate!</u> There is no better time to prove to everyone in a group that you are human as well, than when you join in the fun and play along side them. If you lead problem solving activities later in the training, you will not be able to share this same participatory role. Participating in games builds your credibility and it's great fun!

# INTRODUCTION from Faith

J. Grey said, "The process of learning requires not only learning and applying, but also forgetting and remembering again." And that is what I have done with every game book I've ever read and used. I learn the game, apply it with a group, and then forget about it until I need it again and there it is: different somehow because the client, the goal, the time and place have changed, and hopefully, so have I!

One of the most useful sayings for me when working with a group is, "Count on your ability to be present and to think, rather than to remember and be perfect." Perfection in the facilitation world is less the goal than mastery. A true master is not the one with the most trainees, but the one who creates the most masters. One of the goals of this book is to create more masters.

The following letter is a partial reminder of what many clients want from their facilitators.

## A LETTER TO MY FACILITATOR

*Dear Facilitator,*

*If you want my interest, loyalty, and best efforts as a group member, please take into account that:*

1. *I need a sense of **belonging**: a feeling that I am...*
   a.  *...sincerely welcome; and*
   b.  *...honestly valued for my total authentic self.*

2. *I need to know in some clear detail just **what is expected of me**, so I can work confidently and creatively.*

3. *I need to be **informed**: what I'm not up on, I may be down on.*

4. *I need to have **confidence in you** that is based upon your assurance that you will be:*
   a.  *group focused, yet individually respectful;*
   b.  *flexible and responsive to needs;*
   c.  *giving of recognition when it is due;*

   *d.  physically and emotionally safety conscious, but not stultifying;*

   *e.  offering "Challenge By Choice" rather than pressuring or manipulating;*

   *f.  cognizant that people learn in different ways and at different speeds;*

   *g.  conscious that my physical environment is directly linked to the quality of my participation; and*

   *h.  willing to take the same risks you ask of me.*

*5.  In brief, the situation in which I find myself **must make sense to me** regardless of how much sense it makes to you.*

*Sincerely yours,*
*A game player.*

As some of you read this book, you will say to yourself, "I could have written this!" And it's true. In fact, you may recognize many activities (or versions) that you have done, or have forgotten about doing. Writing a book provides a perfect excuse to take the experiences out of our heads, off the margins of old programs and out of jammed file folders, and put them on paper in an organized and thoughtful way. Our intent is that you (we) feel affirmed and vitalized about continuing to play, to experiment, to invent, to share, and to and explore the ever growing body of knowledge.

The only real concern about writing this book is around ethics: giving credit where credit is due to those who invented activities. Many activities have been "out there and in use" for years and have gone through many transformations to be nearly unrecognizable: a bit like gossip, where the end vaguely resembles the beginning and few know who started it. We are grateful to be standing on the giant shoulders of the game makers who have gone before, and wish for a time machine ride to let us view and appreciate the generous oral tradition which fanned those early sparks. We welcome clarifying information regarding origins of games, and intend to upset or discount no one. Mistakes will be found so please let us know about them and accept our apologies in advance. AND pardon our conversational and sometimes grammatically incorrect use of pronouns such as he, she, I, you, their, etc. Game playing isn't rigid or rule-bound and neither is our language!

# LEGEND

Information for each of the 99 activities is presented in a consistent format. This page explains the typical legend used for each game.

---

## No.         NAME OF THE GAME

**PROPS**: number of props      **SIZE**: number of people
**MOVE**: level of movement     **TYPE**: which categories
**AREA**: recommended area    **ORIGIN**: source/creator
**TIME**: range of time taken     **REFERENCE**: book-pg.

*A DIAGRAM*

*provides visual examples to enhance descriptions*

**Intent**: lists some primary purposes of the game.

**Action**: briefly describes what happens in the game.

**Highlights**: explains special considerations or safety concerns.

**Preparation**: details key equipment and setup procedures.

**Script**: outlines *what the facilitator says* (or actually does) and occasionally may outline how players might typically respond.

**Variations**: gives alternate versions and subtle changes that can be used to make games easier, harder or just plain different.

**PROPS** lists the number of props needed in the game according to this scale:

|  |  |
|---|---|
|  | 1 = only one |
| 0 = none | 2 = two or more |

**MOVE** describes the level of movement in the game according to this scale:

|  |  |
|---|---|
|  | 2 = moderate / walking |
| 0 = none / sitting | 3 = heavy / sweating |
| 1 = light / standing | 4 = extreme / lifting |

**AREA** gives a recommended (inside or outside) space for a game. Large is wide or open enough for your group to run around freely. Medium is sufficient for your group to form a circle and work in it. Small is adequate for individual's or partner's to do "table" work.

**TIME** gives the duration commonly taken to complete each game.

**SIZE** gives an ideal number of people who typically play the game.

**TYPE** explains the primary (written out) and secondary (initials in parentheses) category which this game fits into according to this list:

W = WARMUPS get people's heart rates elevated or stretch their muscles and joints to avoid injuries;

O = OPENERS set the program tone by detailing themes or introducing people to learn their names;

S = SOCIALIZERS deinhibit people or familiarize them, so that they learn more than one another's names;

F = FILLERS occupy unexpected program gaps with more, sedentary and time consuming games;

E = ENERGIZERS quickly motivate, invigorate, or raise levels of enthusiasm through physical activity; and

C = CLOSERS highlight learning, celebrate achievement, or bring new commitments for future change.

**ORIGIN** gives credit to the initial creator or information source.

**REFERENCE** provides the classic book and page number where an original game description can be found (see Simon's introduction for a list of some of these books and their publication details).

# 1                    STRETCHING

**PROPS**: 0 (none)             **SIZE**: Any (individuals)
**MOVE**: 1 (light / standing)  **TYPE**: Warmup (E)
**AREA**: Large                 **ORIGIN**: Yoga & P.E.
**TIME**: 5-15 minutes          **REFERENCE**: BBA-7

| Relax & begin | Arms back | Arms forward | Arms Up | Bend forward |
|:---:|:---:|:---:|:---:|:---:|

| Runner's stretch | Gentle pushup | Arch back |
|:---:|:---:|:---:|

| Arch forward | Runner's stretch | Bend forward | Relax & end |
|:---:|:---:|:---:|:---:|

**Intent**: Loosen muscles / joints, increase flexibility, reduce injury.

**Action**: Individuals stretch by themselves in creative ways.

**Highlights**: The key to stretching is to avoid bouncing and sudden movements. Ask folks to move slowly, smoothly, and deliberately. Encourage them to learn their limits and not to overstretch anything.

**Preparation**: Encourage people to "shake it out" before stretching. When thinking about the order of muscles to stretch, realize that most major joints have two groups of muscles that oppose one another (move the joint in opposite directions). Therefore, start at the bottom of the body (toes) and move upward to the head. Avoid rotating joints (don't roll the neck), simply stretch in a linear fashion (stretch the neck from side to side or forwards and back: no twists).

**Script**: *We are going to stretch a little before we get active. I'd like you to find your own space away from others, and from where you can still see my demonstrations. We will begin with our ankles and work up through knees, hips, back, wrists, elbows, shoulders, and end at the neck. Do NOT bounce or make any sudden moves. You should NOT do this if you feel any unpleasant pains. Move slowly and smoothly. Learn your limits and avoid overdoing any stretch!*

Demonstrate some of these stretches and have people repeat them:

ANKLES: point the toes & stretch calves while standing on a step.
KNEES: straighten legs & stand with one foot held up behind bum.
HIPS: stand straight up, place leg on low table (front, back & side).
BACK: place hands on lower back; lean back (not for weak backs)!
WRISTS: with forearms level, press palm to palm & heel to heel.
ELBOWS: straighten arms & reach OVER shoulders to touch spine.
SHOULDERS: pull arm across chest, & again across behind back.
NECK: look up, look down, tilt head from side to side (no twists).

**Variations**: Refer to a stretching textbook for acceptable exercises. A combination stretch sequence is diagrammed opposite. Do not introduce any new stretches, unless you're certain they are correct.

# 2          PARTNER STRETCHING

**PROPS**: 0 (none)                **SIZE**: Any (partners)
**MOVE**: 1 (light / standing)     **TYPE**: Warmup (O, S, E)
**AREA**: Large                    **ORIGIN**: Classic
**TIME**: 5-15 minutes             **REFERENCE**: BBA-5

Mirrored
Stretching

Resistance
Stretching

**Intent**: Loosen muscles / joints, increase flexibility, reduce injury.

**Action**: Individuals stretch with their partners in creative ways.

**Highlights**: The key to stretching is to avoid bouncing and sudden movements. Ask folks to move slowly, smoothly, and deliberately. Encourage them to learn their limits and to not overstretch anything. Discourage partners from forcibly stretching or moving each other.

**Preparation**: Encourage plenty of individual stretching in advance.

**Script**: *Now that we are loosened up from our own stretching, I'd like you to find a partner. First, just a reminder to take it easy and avoid bouncing, quick jerky moves, or overdoing it. Next, pretend you are a mirror to your partners' stretching and do what they do.*

Partners perform several dramatic mirrored stretching movements.

*Okay, now that you and your partner are well coordinated, I'd like you to try stretching one another. Be careful not to force your partner's joints! In this exercise, one person decides on a common stretching movement and the other provides resistance to that movement. JUST resistance now, NOT additional movement. Any questions?*

Demonstrate: hold your arms straight out in front of you with palms together and, with your partner preventing you from separating your hands, attempt to open your arms against this resistance.

*All right, let's try another. Stand facing one another, extend your straightened arms forward and place your hands palms down on your partner's shoulders. Now push downward as hard as you can and hold for 5 seconds. Relax. Okay push and hold for another 5!*

As partners conduct their resistance stretching, circulate and coach. Be prepared to discourage dangerous choices and "forced" actions.

**Variations**: After warming up the hamstrings, get into groups of 3 or 4 and try a <u>Stork Stretch</u>. While holding hands in a circle, lean back, simultaneously raise your right leg and place it on the raised leg of the neighbor on your right. Repeat for the left legs.

# 3                    GOALS IN SIGHT

**PROPS**: 0 (none)          **SIZE**: Any (individuals)
**MOVE**: 1 (light / standing)   **TYPE**: Warmup (O, E)
**AREA**: Large              **ORIGIN**: Diane Dick
**TIME**: 0-5 minutes        **REFERENCE**: New

**Intent**: With practice, we can stretch farther than we thought.

**Action**: People stand still, twist slowly, and look behind them.

**Highlights**: This is one of the few stretches that involves twisting and so should not be undertaken by people with spinal concerns! Ask folks with back or neck problems to voluntarily sit this one out. Do not let people twist quickly, since this may cause a back injury.

**Preparation**: Demonstrate this stretch before people try it. Have enough space for everybody to stretch without hitting anyone.

**Script**: *Stand comfortably with your feet spread shoulder width apart. Hold your arm straight in front of you and make a "thumbs-up" sign. Sight over your thumb and select an object in front of you. What did you sight on?* People respond.

*Now I'd like you to SLOWLY swing your arm around behind you as far as you can, by twisting at the waist and without moving your feet. Once you have reached your maximum stretch, sight over your thumb again, remember what you saw, and return to the start.*

*Now try that again, very slowly, and go as far as you can. At the farthest point, sight over your thumb once more and return to the start. What did you notice?* People share they were able to go further the second time. *Let's repeat the exercise for the left arm.*

*Much like this exercise, today's program will give you a chance to advance to a place where you are able to do more than you thought you could. It will take stretching and practice, but it is possible!*

**Variations**: The above twist can be done with just the head (rotate the neck and not the body). Here is one more twisting stretch. In Windmills, partners stand back to back and move arms together to mimic a windmill. It requires more coordination than flexibility, but might be risky for people with back, neck, or shoulder problems.

*Pick a partner about the same size as you. Stand back to back with a slight space between partners and your feet shoulder width apart. With hands at your side, loosely hold finger tips and make sure you start this motion slowly and increase your speed as you are ready.*

*Keep your feet stationary. Raise your hands on one side over your heads and down past your waists to touch the ground on the other side. As you do this, your own arm will pass in front of your face.*

*As you return the first pair of hands, and as they pass in front of your face, raise the second pair of hands to follow across and touch the ground on the initial side. Reverse and repeat this very complex process without losing finger tip contact with your partner's hands.*

# 4                          STORY STRETCH

**PROPS**: 0 (none)          **SIZE**: 10-20
**MOVE**: 2 (moderate / walking)   **TYPE**: Warmup (O, E)
**AREA**: Large             **ORIGIN**: Steve Gustafson
**TIME**: 0-5 minutes        **REFERENCE**: New

COUCH
POTATO

**Intent**: Stretch muscles, start moving, and have fun.

**Action**: Facilitator tells an interesting story with stretches built in.

**Highlights**: Two things are very important when you facilitate a story stretch: attitude and a good story. Your enthusiasm and modeling can encourage almost anyone to join in some silliness.

**Preparation**: Gather people in a circle with room to move about. Be prepared to exaggerate movements so people can stretch well.

**Script**:*What comes to mind when I say "couch potato?"* People give various responses. *Studies have shown that more and more couch potatoes are sprouting up every year. Bigger entertainment centers, the Internet, and various energy saving devices have helped the situation along. So in the interest of helping these people, here is the Couch Potato Stretch. Please do as I do and follow along.*

*Tap your right thigh. Pick up your leg to have a seat on the sofa* (stand with your knees slightly bent and your upper body slightly back and relaxed). *Stretch your right arm way out and reach for the TV remote. Stretch that right thumb* (act like you are pushing the remote buttons). *Okay, nothing's on! Reach out with your left arm and get the VCR remote. Fast forward...rewind....* (push buttons with your left thumb). *Oh! Pause.... I love that scene! Okay, keep searching. Nothing more worthwhile, put the remote down.*

*Tap your left thigh. Stand up off the couch. Let's go to the kitchen for a snack. Step...step...step....* (make very exaggerated walking movements). *Watch out for the trash and clothes on the floor* (add high steps over precious objects). *Oh oh, I think we stepped in some pizza! Okay, wipe your feet.* (make doormat motions). *Good enough, on to the kitchen. Step...step...step....*

*Okay, there it is. Some folks call it a refrigerator, others call it the "tower of power!" Right hand out, open the door. Oops, it opens the other way. Left hand out, open the door. Up on your tip toes to look for something on the top shelf. Nope, don't see it. Bend down and look for it on the bottom shelf. Reach in and move the lettuce out of the way* (add suitable movements). *Nope, still don't see it. Okay, back to the top shelf* (up on tip toes again).

*THERE IT IS!!!! Way in the back! Reach in, get it, pull it out, and shut the door. Pop the top, hold it way over your head, and chug it down!* Continue the story from there or ask others to contribute.

**Variations:** Another story stretch was created by the local sheriff's department. They call it the <u>Hold-up Stretch</u>: you are being mugged by someone behind you. *Reach for the sky!* (slowly put both hands in the air). *Give me your wallet!* (slowly reach down with your left hand into your right pocket). *Hands up!* (slowly put your hands back up). *Where's that money?* (slowly reach down with your right hand to check your left pocket). *Hands up again!* (once more slowly into the air). *You hear a noise and then all is quiet. You carefully look over your left shoulder and then your right one. You slowly lower your hands to your knees and look through your legs. The robber appears to be gone! Shake it out and relax....*

Have others make up parts of a story and put the stretches together.

# 5            MRS. GRADY STRETCH

**PROPS**: 0 (none)                    **SIZE**: 10-20
**MOVE**: 2 (moderate / walking)       **TYPE**: Warmup (O, E)
**AREA**: Large                        **ORIGIN**: Classic
**TIME**: 5-15 minutes                 **REFERENCE**: SB-180

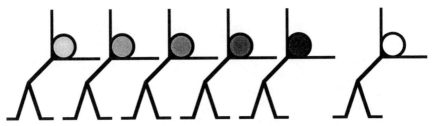

Mrs. Grady was promoted for doing THIS!

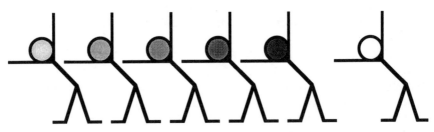

Mrs. Grady was promoted for doing THAT!

**Intent**: Stretching, coaching, communication, and learning names.

**Action**: Each person in the group leads one stretching movement.

**Highlights**: Start this one without an introduction. Begin right away with the script below. Pick a supportive person to follow you and the group will almost always complete one round of the circle.

**Preparation**: Gather the group into a circle with enough space so people can move and swing their arms without hitting anyone.

**Script**: *Hey Bill!* (call the name of the person to your right). *Did you hear about Mrs. Grady?*

Bill answers; "No!"

*She got promoted for doing THIS....* Demonstrate a stretching movement of your choice and encourage others to try it. Then coach Bill (or that person to your right) to repeat this with the next person in the circle.

Bill (or that person) now says to the next person; Hey Sally! Did you hear about Mrs. Grady?

Sally answers; "No!"

She got promoted for doing this.... Bill demonstrates a chosen stretch and everyone repeats it.

The pattern continues with Sally until everyone has contributed a stretch movement. You may need to support people who can't think of a movement by asking the group for their suggestions.

**Variations**: Change the name of the character. Change promotion to another positive or negative event. After each new stretch has been added, repeat all the previous ones in order as well.

# 6                        COUNTERBALANCE

**PROPS**: 0 (none)              **SIZE**: Any (partners)
**MOVE**: 4 (extreme / lifting)  **TYPE**: Warmup (O, S, E)
**AREA**: Large                  **ORIGIN**: Classic
**TIME**: 0-5 minutes            **REFERENCE**: BPA-96

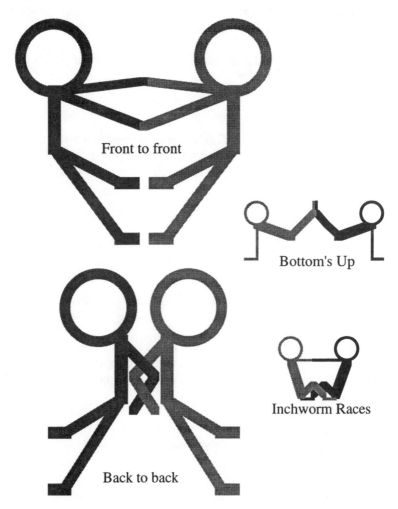

Front to front

Bottom's Up

Back to back

Inchworm Races

**Intent**: Stretching, working together, trust, support and movement.

**Action**: Partners counterbalance and support each other as they sit down and stand up, while facing one another or while back to back.

**Highlights**: Encourage slow, smooth, and deliberate movement.

**Preparation**: Make sure people are well stretched before trying this one. Offer the option to watch or coach rather than participate.

**Script**: *Find a partner about your size and turn to face each other. Hold hands and lean back with your feet touching toe to toe with your partner's feet. Remaining in this trust position, slowly sit down while mutually supporting one another.*

*Now that you are seated, move your feet underneath your body and try to stand up again, while still holding hands and leaning back. Help support each other and push with your legs at the same time.*

*For those who are willing, repeat this sequence by standing back to back and by locking arms. Be very careful not to pull too hard and overpower your partner on the way down and back up. Keep your balance by pushing your backs against one another.*

**Variations**: If it worked in pairs, the same may work for groups of 4 or more. See how many you can include. Try these options.

In <u>Bottom's Up</u>, two or four people sit on the ground with their palms on the ground behind and beside them. Facing their partners, they press the soles of their feet together and lift their bottoms off the ground. With four, pay close attention to arranging their feet.

In <u>Popsicle Pushups</u>, four people do a classic pushup (or preferred variation) with the feet of their neighbor placed comfortably on their own back or legs and everyone pushes up together at the same time.

<u>Inchworm Races</u> are great games to follow these warmups, but they involve close contact, so think carefully about a group's readiness. *Sit on the ground facing your partner with your feet together and your toes touching the toes of your partner. Shuffle forward until you are sitting on top of your partner's feet and your partner is on yours. Now grab behind each other's elbows with your hands and pull. Rock back and forth until you begin moving like inchworms!*

# 7                          TEAM TOE TOUCH

**PROPS**: 0 (none)               **SIZE**: 20-50
**MOVE**: 1 (light / standing)    **TYPE**: Warmup (O, S, E)
**AREA**: Large                   **ORIGIN**: Classic
**TIME**: 5-15 minutes            **REFERENCE**: New

**Intent**: Alternative stretching, group involvement, and listening.

**Action**: Group does stretching movements in a tight circle.

**Highlights**: In addition to typical stretching cautions, encourage people with back and/or knee injuries to adapt what they do.

**Preparation**: Encourage some individual stretching beforehand.

**Script**: *Form a circle close enough so that your feet are shoulder width apart, touching the feet of the neighbor on either side of you.*

*Raise both hands high into the air and stretch your body well.*

*Now drop your left hand and keep your right hand up. Slowly lower your right hand and touch your left toes. Feel free to bend at the knees in order to make this work.* Repeat for other hand.

*Raise both hands. Drop your right hand; keep your left hand up. Slowly lower your left hand and touch your right neighbor's left toes. Again, bend where you need in order to make this work.* Repeat for the LEFT hand and the LEFT neighbor's RIGHT toes.

*Both hands up. Drop your right hand; keep your left hand up. Slowly lower your left hand and touch your right neighbor's right toes. Use each other for support if you need to.* Repeat for the LEFT hand and the LEFT neighbor's LEFT toes.

*Hands up. Slowly lower your arms to the back of your neighbors on either side of you. Slowly look over your right shoulder; now look over your left shoulder; then face forward.*

*Now supporting the people on both sides of you, slowly look up and back as far as you can without falling over.*

*Come back to the center and slowly let go. Relax. Shake it out!*

**Variations:** Depending on the physical abilities of a group, this stretch sequence can be made easier by asking people to touch their neighbors ankles or knees.

# 8 CONNECTIONS

**PROPS**: 0 (none)
**MOVE**: 2 (moderate / walking)
**AREA**: Large
**TIME**: 0-5 minutes

**SIZE**: Any (partners)
**TYPE**: Warmup (O, S, E)
**ORIGIN**: Unknown
**REFERENCE**: MNG-165

Forehead to forehead;
elbow to elbow;
knee to knee; and
MAKE CONNECTIONS!

**Intent**: Stretch, interact, trust, deinhibit, familiarize one another.

**Action**: Partners physically connect as designated by a caller and then move on to a new partner.

**Highlights**: Although you start this game, the caller changes with each round. Since new callers get to choose the connection points, be aware that some callers may choose inappropriate connections.

**Preparation**: This game works best with odd numbers of people so that everyone has a partner except the extra person, who is the caller. With even numbers, ask two people to play as one, so there will always be one unpartnered individual to be the new caller.

**Script**: *Find a partner! I'll be the caller to begin. In our business, we are always trying to make connections with others. Here is your opportunity to practice making a few of these connections.*

*As caller, my job is to call out pairs of body parts for you and your partner to connect together. For example, if I said "hand to hand" you would connect one of your hands to one of your partner's hands. While you maintain the connection, I might call another set. Let's say it is "right foot to left foot!" Try that as well. While still holding those two connections I might still ask you to connect "ear to ear!" Some positions can become uncomfortable, so I'll call out "MAKE CONNECTIONS!" When you hear that call, disconnect from your partner and quickly find a new one.*

*The person without a partner becomes the caller for the next round. Please keep connections reasonable and G-rated. Any questions?*

**Variations:** Put pieces of paper listing body parts into a hat and ask people to draw out two pieces that can be connected. After three connections, yell "make connections" and repeat the process.

# 9                              ROPE JOUSTING

**PROPS**: 1 (one only)        **SIZE**: 1-10 (partners)
**MOVE**: 3 (heavy / moving)   **TYPE**: Warmup (O, S, E)
**AREA**: Medium               **ORIGIN**: Outward Bound
**TIME**: 5-15 minutes         **REFERENCE**: CC-72

**Intent**: Movement, quick thinking, strategizing, and competition.

**Action**: Partners tug on a rope attempting to unbalance each other.

**Highlights**: Do this after people have stretched and warmed up. Diminish the importance of winning and enhance to value of fun.

**Preparation**: Obtain a 60' piece of rope for each partnership. Be sure the open area is free of obstacles with a soft landing surface. Ask people to pair up and face their partners with about 30' of space between them. Lay out the untangled rope so that one end is at the feet of each person and most of the rope is spread between them.

**Script**: *When I say READY, stand facing one another with your feet together. When I say STEADY, pick up the rope end at your feet. When I say GO, take in all the slack, and yank or release the rope as necessary to unbalance your partner by getting his or her feet to move. Letting go of the rope counts as being unbalanced. Any questions? READY, assume your stance. STEADY, pick up the rope. GO!*

**Variations**: Have people stand inside 3' diameter circles. Foot movements are allowed, but not outside the marked circle. For larger groups, people can work together on the same end of the rope. Here are several alternative paired games.

The Bends also involves two people attempting to get the other to lose balance. In this activity they stand on one foot and hold their other foot off the ground with one hand. With their open hand, they shake hands with their partner, and push or pull causing the other to move a standing foot or let go of their held foot.

Squat Thrust is similar to the above, but partners squat down facing one another and do NOT lock hands. Instead, they place palms to palms and attempt to thrust each other off balance. Since the above variations are over quickly, encourage people to try many partners.

Can't Touch Me is a non-contact version, where people stand toe to toe (leading with one foot in front of the other) and attempt to knock the other off balance, but without physically touching one another.

# 10          TWENTY TYPES OF TAG

**PROPS**: 0 (none)
**MOVE**: 3 (heavy / moving)
**AREA**: Large
**TIME**: 15-30 minutes

**SIZE**: Any
**TYPE**: Warmup (O, S, E)
**ORIGIN**: Classic
**REFERENCE**: New

**Intent**: Elevate people's heart rates and have lots of fun!

**Action**: People chaotically pursue one another around open spaces.

**Highlights**: Tag games can cause injuries by people getting carried away with excitement and beginning to run or tackle. Ask people to walk and NOT run or, if this in unrealistic, teach "SHUFFLING" skills as an alternative to walking and running. Play tag after stretching first. Manage safety in crowds by playing for shorter periods and in smaller spaces that prevent people from getting up to a high speed and running into one another. Encourage tagging by gentle touch; discourage slapping and tackling!

**Preparation**: Be sure the open area used is free from dangerous obstacles. You may want to identify a safe zone (where observers can watch from a distance). If playing a "freezing" game, decide in advance if "unfreezing" will be allowed. Also choose whether the tagged individuals (or group) will need to spin around (360 degrees once, twice, or thrice) before pursuing during their turn to tag.

**Script**: *Before we do this next activity, I'd like to teach you how to shuffle. Shuffling involves never breaking contact between the ground and your feet as you move* (demonstrate a good shuffle). *Therefore, walking and running are NOT shuffling, because the feet leave the ground. In this next activity, we WILL be shuffling instead of running and/or walking* (you may want to share a consequence for people who might walk or run). *Any questions? Okay, here are game rules and some safety concerns.... GO!*

**Variations**: Instead of touching, throwing SOFT objects (fleece balls or rolled up socks) can be substituted for contact tagging. The soft objects can also be tossed for immunity to someone about to be tagged. Here are 20 types of tag, starting with an old favorite.

1. You're IT! Pick one person to be the tagger and to pursue all the other tagees. Once another person gets tagged, he or she becomes IT and assumes the tagging role from the previous person. To prevent immediate retagging, ask people to count to 5 with eyes closed, hop up and down for 3 seconds, or spin around on the spot a few times before staring to pursue others.

2.   <u>Everybody's IT!</u>  Pick everyone present to be IT.  If you get tagged by another, simply sit down or stand to the side.  If dispute occur as to who got tagged first: both are out!  Since elimination games may be discriminatory, simply shout "GO" again and keep the game moving.

3.   <u>Partner Tag</u>.  Ask everyone to find a partner.  Ask partners to choose one person to be IT; the other to be pursued.  Count to ten (giving them time to spread out) before shouting GO!

4.   <u>Cyclops Tag</u>.  Slow movement is extremely important in this activity so reemphasize the need for shuffling.  Like partner tag, but everyone closes one eye and looks through a circled hand held to their other eye to create tunnel vision.  People will bump into one another while pursuing, so encourage them to move slowly and use their other free hand to feel their way.

5.   <u>Pairs Tag</u>.  Ask everyone to stand beside another person and link arms (or hold hands).  Select a pair to be IT, pick the type of tag to play, and then have the pair pursue all the other pairs.

6.   <u>Squares Tag</u>.  Ask each pair to find and join with another pair by holding hands in a square.  Pick some squares to be IT and to pursue all the other squares according to the chosen rules.

7.   <u>Triangle Tag</u>.  Ask a square to pick one person to be IT and to step out leaving the others to form a triangle.  Then ask them to pick another person for IT to try and tag.  IT pursues this person, while the triangle continually reorients its position to block tagging.  Rotate roles in the group to maintain interest.

8.   <u>Add-On Tag</u>.  An individual, pair, or square is chosen IT and is pursuing all others.  However, when tagged this time, the others join to make an ever growing IT, until only one remains untagged.  Instead of celebrating survivors, shout GO!

9.   <u>Hospital Tag</u>.  Play your choice of tag game, but when people get tagged, they are required to hold the place on their bodies where they were tagged with one hand and continue playing.  When tagged a second time, they also hold the second place, leaving them unable to use their hands for tagging or moving.

10.   <u>Elbow Tag</u>. Ask everyone to find partners and link arms with hands on hips. Separate one partnership to begin, and pick one person (IT) to pursue the other. Explain that one way to obtain immunity (and thus escape IT) is to join a partnership by linking arms with a partner on one end. This forces the partner on the other end to leave the partnership and become the newly pursued until finding another partnership to join.

11.   <u>Frozen Tag</u>. Played with two groups in competition. Tagged people are stuck in place with their feet far apart. They can be unfrozen only by a group member crawling through their legs.

12.   <u>Transformer Tag</u>. Two teams (designated by a hand on heads or hand on tails) attempt to tag and convert others to their side.

13.   <u>Clothespin Tag</u>. Each person gets 5 springloaded clothespins. The task is to get rid of all 5 pins by clipping them to others' backs. If clipped, remove pins from your back to clip again.

14.   <u>Bean Bag Tag</u>. Play a chosen tag game while balancing bean bags on heads. If a bag falls off, its the same as being tagged.

15.   <u>Blindfolded Tag</u>. Vary any tag game by blindfolding people. Obviously, each person needs a helper to tell them what to do.

16.   <u>Piggyback Tag</u>. Like any tag game, but immunity from being tagged is given to two people assuming a piggyback position.

17.   <u>Flamingo Tag</u>. For immunity, people stand like a flamingo: holding one leg up behind them with one of their hands and making a bird-like beak with the other hand on their forehead.

18.   <u>Name Tag</u>. IT's must call out correct names of people they tag or the tag doesn't count. Practice learning names first.

19.   <u>Slow Tag</u>. Group members count cadence for their shuffling.

20.   <u>Toe Tag</u>. Tagging is conducted by very aerobic "toe fencing!" Pairs hold hands and tap the top of their partner's shoe with bottom of their shoes. After three successful toe tags, both partners go in search of new partnerships and repeat the game.

# 11                              NAME ROULETTE

**PROPS**: 0 (none)                    **SIZE**: 10-20
**MOVE**: 1 (light / standing)         **TYPE**: Opener (S, F, E)
**AREA**: Medium                       **ORIGIN**: Lee Gillis
**TIME**: 15-30 minutes                **REFERENCE**: BPA-70

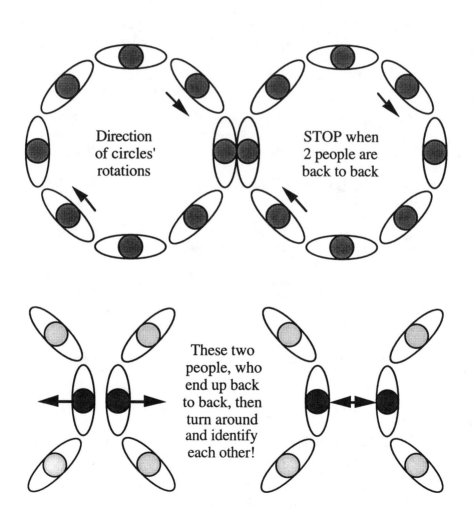

Direction of circles' rotations

STOP when 2 people are back to back

These two people, who end up back to back, then turn around and identify each other!

**Intent**: Learn names, have fun, and relax.

**Action**: People turn around and name the person opposite them.

**Highlights**: Much laughter ensues when people recognize the other person, but can't seem to quickly recall his or her name.

**Preparation**: Form two adjacent circles of roughly equal size with people facing inwards and with a person from each circle standing back to back. If wearing name tags, temporarily remove them.

**Script**: *When I say GO, begin rotating your circle. Both circles turn clockwise* (or counterclockwise) *with people looking forward into the center. When I call STOP, the circles will stop rotating and people will remain facing the center. When I call LOOK, only the two people in these positions* (indicate those two who are back to back) *will turn around to look at each other. The first person to correctly call out the name of the other person invites that other person to change circles. The game ends when one group dissolves or time expires. Any questions?*

*GO!      STOP!      LOOK!      Please move over to this group.*

**Variations**: <u>Peak-a-who</u> involves two groups separated by a large vertically suspended opaque blanket. When the blanket is raised, each group selects a member to sit facing the blanket (with the other group's selection on the other side). When the blanket is dropped, the two selected members (or the whole group) call out the other's name. The last one to get the name correct, joins the other group.

In both Name Roulette and Peek-a-who, have people stay back to back and guess the names based on clues provided by their group. Either game can be played to music (like musical chairs). When the music stops, people turn around or the blanket is lifted. For groups where first and last names are known, use middle or nicknames.

# 12        NO PROPS NAME TOSS

**PROPS**: 0 (none)                    **SIZE**: 1-10
**MOVE**: 2 (moderate / walking)       **TYPE**: Opener (S, F, E)
**AREA**: Medium                       **ORIGIN**: Karl Rohnke
**TIME**: 5-15 minutes                 **REFERENCE**: FSI-8

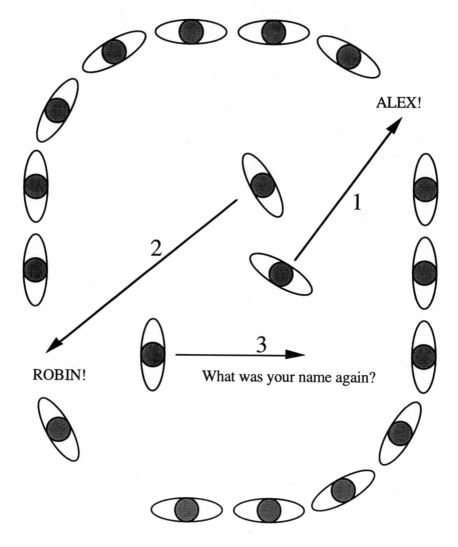

**Intent**: Learn names, have fun, and relax.

**Action**: People change places around a circle by calling out names.

**Highlights**: A classic and well used activity is Toss, where people throw a ball around a circle in order to learn names (see #1 in "101 Corporate Teambuilding Activities" or SB-17 and BBA-8). Use this version when you don't have something for people to throw.

**Preparation**: Ask people to form a circle about elbow length apart. You may find it easier to be a member of the group circle to begin. If wearing name tags, ask people to temporarily remove them.

**Script**: *In this game we will be trading places with people across the circle from us as we call out their names. If you don't know a name, feel free to ask.*

*I'll begin by stepping into the circle, making eye contact with a person in the circle, and calling him or her by name: DANA! The second you hear your name, you will vacate your space, so the incoming person (me) can occupy it. You then step into the circle, make eye contact, and call out another name: KIM! And so on.*

*The game ends when we know everyone's names. Any questions?*

**Variations**: For greater challenge, have more than one person changing places at a time. Start off with two or three. As the circle gets crowded, remind folks to avoid collisions.

People can shake hands as they pass across the circle and can thank the person who called them by name: THANK YOU, LINDSAY!

For groups where names are well known, use middle or nicknames. This game can always be played in the classic style by tossing balls.

# 13   ALPHABETICAL NAME CIRCLE

**PROPS**: 0 (none)
**MOVE**: 2 (moderate / walking)
**AREA**: Medium
**TIME**: 5-15 minutes

**SIZE**: 20-50
**TYPE**: Opener (S, F, E)
**ORIGIN**: Steve Butler
**REFERENCE**: QS-92

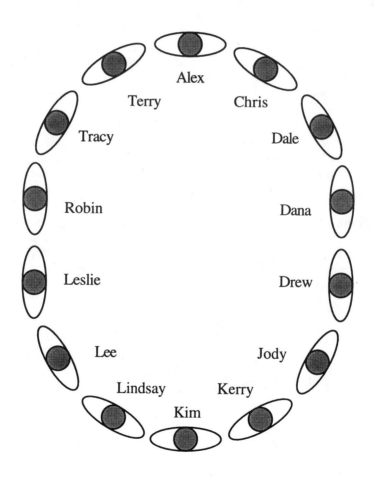

**Intent**: Learn names, have fun, nonverbal communication.

**Action**: People place themselves in order around a circle by names.

**Highlights**: A classic and well used activity is Line-ups, where people form a sequenced line according to key criteria: age, height, etc. (see #44 in "101 Corporate Teambuilding Activities" or SB-163 and BBA-98). This alphabetical name version is done in a circle.

**Preparation**: Ask people to form a circle about elbow length apart. You may find it easier to be a member of the group circle to begin. If wearing name tags, ask people to temporarily remove them.

**Script**: *Let's go once around the circle saying our names proudly and loudly. I'll start.* People share their names. *Excellent, we all seem to know that part really well! Now we can get more complex.*

*This next activity is done nonverbally: without speaking. I'd like you to arrange yourselves in a circle by alphabetical order according to the letter of your first* (or last) *name and without talking!* People mix up, move around, communicate nonverbally, and eventually reform the circle.

*If you are ready and think you are in the correct place, please raise your arm.* (Once the vast majority of arms are raised), *okay, let's go around again saying our names and see how we did. Who wants to go first?* People share their names. Repeat as necessary until people are satisfied. When finished, encourage them to say hello and introduce themselves to their neighbors on either side.

**Variations**: For groups where first or last names are already very well known, use middle names or have people make up nicknames. If the circle presents a barrier, use the classic linear version.

# 14                     NAME EXCHANGE

**PROPS**: 1 (one only)              **SIZE**: Any (individuals)
**MOVE**: 2 (moderate / walking)     **TYPE**: Opener (S, F, E)
**AREA**: Medium                     **ORIGIN**: Unknown
**TIME**: 0-5 minutes                **REFERENCE**: New

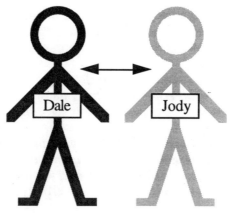

Hi!  Your name is now Dale          Hello! and you are now Jody

Hi!  Your        Hello! and
name is          you can be
now Drew         called Jody

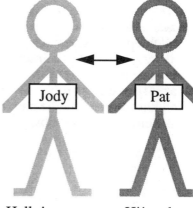

Hello! your      Hi! and
name is          you can
now Dale         become Pat

**Intent**: Learn names for later on, have fun, interact and socialize.

**Action**: People meet and greet, then the room gets noisy.

**Highlights**: Play this early in a program. People are unlikely to recall every name, but may recognize and remember names later on.

**Preparation**: Name tags not needed. When noisy, you may want to use a whistle in order to get folks' attention.

**Script**: *Hello everyone. I know some of you have not had a chance to meet everyone in the room, so you will have that opportunity in this activity called "Name Exchange!"*

*In this activity, you select and approach someone you don't yet know. After greeting them, perhaps with a handshake or a hello, you introduce yourself by sharing your name. Listen carefully to the person's name because you will take that name as your own to the next introduction. At the next introduction, use your new name when greeting the next person and then exchange names again.*

*If you get your own name back, you can pass it on again. Meet as many people as you can in five minutes. Any questions? GO!*

People meet and greet one another and swap names for 5 minutes.

*STOP! Okay, now I'd like you to introduce yourself aloud using the name you are currently holding. Who would like to go first?....*

**Variations**: People can exchange greetings as well as names. You can also check to see who "belongs" to the names that are called out and who else recalls having had that name once during the game.

# 15　　　　INTRODUCTIONS

**PROPS**: 1 (one only)　　　**SIZE**: Any (individuals)
**MOVE**: 1 (light / standing)　**TYPE**: Opener (S, F, E)
**AREA**: Large　　　　　　**ORIGIN**: Unknown
**TIME**: 0-5 minutes　　　　**REFERENCE**: New

?: LEE, I'd like you to meet KERRY;
and KERRY, this is LEE!

**Intent**: Interact and socialize, but NOT necessarily learn names.

**Action**: People introduce people, not themselves, to other people.

**Highlights**: If you model this game with energy and enthusiasm, then people will participate with energy and enthusiasm. This game can relieve the tension of meeting strangers or being in a new place.

**Preparation**: Gather everyone together. You may want a whistle in order to get folks' attention when the activity gets very noisy.

**Script**: *Your job is to introduce everyone else to everyone else in 5 minutes without ever introducing yourself. Someone else will do that for you! It might look something like this* (energetically walk across the circle, greet someone and ask their name). *Lee!*

*Then take that person by the arm and find a second person* (move quickly to another section of the circle, greet another person and ask their name). *Kerry! Once you know both names, introduce them to each other. Lee, I'd like you to meet Kerry. Kerry, this is Lee!*

(Emphasize) *notice that Lee and Kerry smiled, spoke one another's names, and greeted with a handshake and a "hello!"* (encourage applause). *Once this introduction is over, all three of us can walk away and introduce other people. Notice I didn't introduce myself. Your job is to introduce everybody to everybody. Someone else will introduce you. Don't be concerned with remembering all the names. Simply keep on introducing people. Any questions? GO!*

**Variations**: This activity can be done snowball style, where people wait for someone to introduce them before they introduce others, or can be a free for all, with everyone introducing from the word GO!

If you want to focus on learning names, ask people to return and find everyone they introduced (or met) and learn their names by using them in a sentence or repeating each name 5 times.

# 16   LET ME INTRODUCE MYSELF

**PROPS**: 0 (none)                    **SIZE**: 10-20
**MOVE**: 2 (moderate / walking)       **TYPE**: Opener (S, F, E)
**AREA**: Medium                       **ORIGIN**: Marta Harrison
**TIME**: 5-15 minutes                 **REFERENCE**: FSIII-18

JOH

NA

THON

or

JOHN!

**Intent**: Learn names, stretch, and get the blood flowing.

**Action**: People show a movement for each syllable in their name.

**Highlights**: Associating the syllable sounds and movements can be an effective and enjoyable way to remember names.

**Preparation**: Groups of about 10 are ideal, because each person repeats the sounds and movements of all the people before them.

**Script**: *Let's get into a small circle. Think of the name you like to be called, and how many syllables are in that name. For example, if I wanted to be called "JOHNATHON", there would be three syllables; if I wanted to be called "JOHN", there would be just one.*

*Now think of a movement to accompany the sound of each syllable in your name. "JOH—NA—THON!"* (put your right fist in air, put both hands on hips, and put left fist in air) *or "JOHN!"* (put both fists in the air) *might work for my example. We need simple and interesting movements that we can all repeat. Now think of yours and nod when you have one.*

(When everyone is ready), *okay, I'll start and we'll go around the circle this way* (indicate the direction). *The next person in line will repeat all the sounds and movements before them and add their contribution to the sequence. Questions?*

**Variations**: Have the group repeat each sound and movement in unison, like an instant replay, rather than building the sequence one at a time. After one round, have people mix their circle locations and then go around again with the new order. For stretching, have people choose stretching exercises for their movements. If names are already well known, try using middle names or nicknames.

# 17               FIND YOUR PARTNER

**PROPS**: 2 (two or more)      **SIZE**: 20-50 (partners)
**MOVE**: 2 (moderate / walking) **TYPE**: Opener (S, F, E)
**AREA**: Large                 **ORIGIN**: Karl Rohnke
**TIME**: 5-15 minutes          **REFERENCE**: SB-98

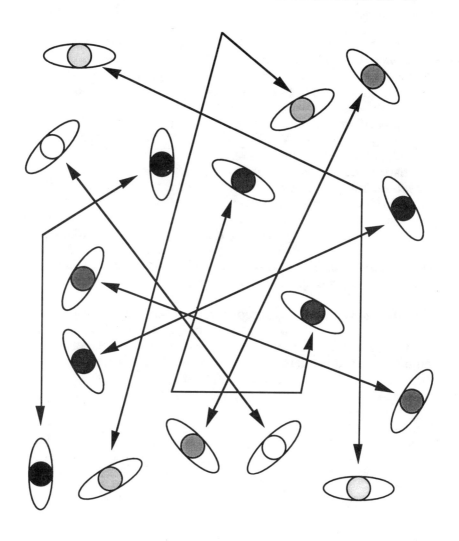

**Intent**: Lower tension, raise energy, make noise, and have fun.

**Action**: Blindfolded partners unite by shouting names in a crowd.

**Highlights**: As partners reunite, they cease calling and the noise decreases so the remainder can hear and find each other.

**Preparation**: Provide a blindfold per person, or ask them to close their eyes and avoid peeking for this activity. This activity is very noisy with large groups, so agree in advance on a signal for STOP! You might want to use a whistle in order to get folks' attention.

**Script**: *Find a partner and introduce yourselves.* People do this. *I'd like you to take turns shouting your own names, as loudly as you can, in order to familiarize yourselves with your partner's voice and name. Take 60 seconds to practice.* People do this.

*Now, leave each other and go to opposite sides of this area and put on your blindfolds.* People do this.

*When I say GO, you are to begin shouting your own name and start listening for your partner. Your task is to reunite with your partner. For safety, remember to keep your hands up in front of you* (called bumpers up) *as you walk. Remove your blindfold only in case of an emergency or once the activity is completed.*

*When you finally find your original partner, celebrate, remove your blindfolds, and silently observe the others. Any questions? GO!*

**Variations**: Instead of shouting your own name, try shouting your partner's name. Instead of names, choose one of these alternatives.

Similar Noises like sounds that animals make or types of machines.
Halves of Words like Peanut & Butter or Pea & Nut or Butt & Er.
Body Music like stepping, smacking, clapping or finger snapping.
Favorite Foods like Salt & Pepper, Toast & Jam, or Salsa & Chips.
Songs like "Row Row Row Your Boat;" both sing the same song.

# 18  CROSSWORD PEOPLE

**PROPS**: 2 (two or more)
**MOVE**: 0 (none / sitting)
**AREA**: Small
**TIME**: 5-15 minutes

**SIZE**: 20-50
**TYPE**: Opener (S, F, C)
**ORIGIN**: Classic
**REFERENCE**: New

|   |   |   |   |   |   |   |   |   |   |
|---|---|---|---|---|---|---|---|---|---|
|   |   |   |   |   |   |   |   |   |   |
|   |   |   |   |   |   | S | A | M |   |
|   |   |   |   |   |   | I |   |   |   |
|   |   |   | F |   |   | M |   |   |   |
|   | T | E | A | M | W | O | R | K |   |
|   |   |   | I |   |   | N |   |   |   |
|   |   |   | T |   |   |   |   |   |   |
|   |   |   | H |   |   |   |   |   |   |
|   |   |   |   |   |   |   |   |   |   |
|   |   |   |   |   |   |   |   |   |   |

Add your name to intersect the crossword

**Intent**: Signing in for a program, learning a few names in advance.

**Action**: People place their names (or keywords) on a crossword.

**Highlights**: This activity gives early arrivers and those standing in line to register something productive to do while they wait.

**Preparation**: You will need some large flip chart or butcher's paper and several colored markers. With a light background color, draw a matrix of squares on the paper like a giant Scrabble board (at least 20 X 20 = 400 squares). Write the word WELCOME (or the program theme or the company name) across the matrix writing one letter per square. Then add your name to the matrix in a way that it intersects with the first word in a crossword style. Write a clear invitation for people to contribute their names in the same style on the matrix. Hang the "ready to write" crossword on a nearby wall.

**Script**: As they enter the room, people add their own names, writing one letter per square, while building from the letters already present on the matrix. Continue until all have contributed a name.

**Variations**: For a closing activity, use the same collection of names created at the start of the program, but ask folks to add words that best describe their experience of the program. Post the "Crossword People" chart in the office as tangible reinforcement.

# 19                GIVE ME A HAND

**PROPS**: 0 (none)
**MOVE**: 1 (light / standing)
**AREA**: Medium
**TIME**: 0-5 minutes

**SIZE**: 50-100
**TYPE**: Opener (S, F, E)
**ORIGIN**: Craig Dobkin
**REFERENCE**: New

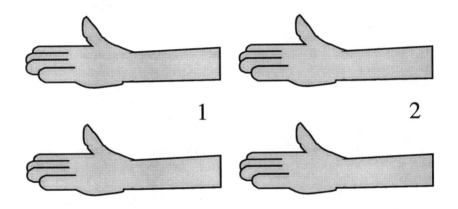

1                                        2

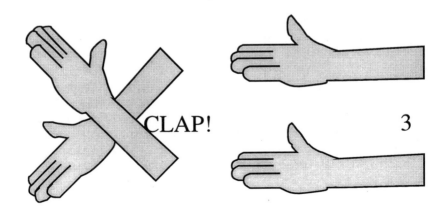

CLAP!

3

**Intent**: Focus, timing, simple small things can have a big impact.

**Action**: People clap in unison as directed by the facilitator.

**Highlights**: Start slowly. Moving too quickly can ruin the effect. Try clapping on three before moving on to more complex motions.

**Preparation**: You should be well visible and audible to everyone. Stand with your arms extended forwards, but turn sideways to all.

**Script**: *I want everyone to watch my hands carefully. When they pass each other, I want you to clap. Let's try* (VERY slowly swing your hands like scissors and make sure the audience claps in unison just as the hands pass by one another). *Okay, I think we've got it.*

*Let's try it all together. Ready?* (stand at the ready position and count). *1...2...3!* (PAUSE, then pass your arms LONG after 3 and note how many clapped on 3 rather than when you moved). *No, I don't think we quite have it yet. We need some more practice* (repeat until no one claps on 3 and all clap when your hands pass).

*All right, that's really good. Let's try another one. Ready?* (stand at the ready position and count). *1...* (then suddenly pass your hands and see who is really paying attention and who is waiting for...) *2...3! We need to practice this some more* (repeat until no one waits for 3 and everyone claps when your hands pass early).

*Okay, we've mastered counting, so we won't need the numbers anymore. We can just continue...* (this time act like your hands will be passing, but stop short and note how many clap). *Ready? Here we go now...* Continue to challenge the group with options.

**Variations**: Here is a list of options: slow-motion hand crossing, claps starting slowly and accelerating like a train, split the audience in half and have one side clap when you face left and the other side clap when you face right, "Shave and a Hair Cut" rhythm, dueling banjos, and swing one arm like playing an electric guitar. Use more facilitators to create rhythmic songs with several parts of the group.

# 20                          SIX COUNT

**PROPS**: 0 (none)
**MOVE**: 3 (heavy / moving)
**AREA**: Large
**TIME**: 0-5 minutes

**SIZE**: 50-100
**TYPE**: Opener (S, F, E)
**ORIGIN**: John Irvin
**REFERENCE**: EM-4

**SIX COUNT**                viewed from infront (facing others)

**Intent**: It is okay to make mistakes, exercising the voice and brain.

**Action**: People raise and lower their arms while counting to six.

**Highlights**: This is a good game to follow physical stretching. The 6-count actually "stretches" the voice and brain. Don't take too much time with it: keep moving and stay in control of the group. Groups seem to hear instructions better after Six Count, because it gets them focused on accomplishing the same task at the same time.

**Preparation**: This game involves a lot of arm swinging so make sure people are well stretched beforehand. You will need to practice the complex movements yourself before leading the group. Be sure you can do them slowly and quickly without having to concentrate.

**Script**: *Does anyone know how to do a 6-count? It goes 1, 2, 3, 4, 5, 6! Let's do it again with "feeling!"* (slowly count from 1 to 6 with everyone at the same time). *1...2...3...4...5...6. Great!*

*Now let's put some action to the count by moving your LEFT hand above your head and down to your side. Your hand goes up on 1, 3, 5; and down on 2, 4, 6.* Repeat the count with the movements.

*Give your left arm a rest and let's give a movement to your RIGHT arm. It goes up on 1, straight out to the side on 2, down on 3, up on 4, straight out to the side on 5, and down on 6. It makes a triangle shape.* Repeat the count with feeling and the movements.

*Now, as if you hadn't guessed, we will put both the arm actions together with the count. Your left arm still goes up and down while your right arm still goes up, out, and down. Any questions?*

Go very slow to begin with and speed up as they learn their moves.

**Variations**: Make up your own new combination of these moves.

# 21                                   SIMON SAYS!

**PROPS**: 0 (none)                     **SIZE**: Any (individuals)
**MOVE**: 3 (heavy / moving)            **TYPE**: Opener (S, F, E)
**AREA**: Large                         **ORIGIN**: Faith Evans
**TIME**: 5-15 minutes                  **REFERENCE**: New

SIMON SAYS
jump up!

come down
OOPS!

**Intent**: You can't learn from mistakes you never make.

**Action**: People play the traditional game Simon Says with a twist.

**Highlights**: A familiar game like Simon Says may ease watchful or guarded tendencies by encouraging participation. People often wonder what is safe and acceptable in a new environment and welcome the opportunity to laugh and play along, regardless of the errors they may make. This is a good one for celebrating mistakes.

**Preparation**: Create a safe atmosphere where mistakes are taken lightly and even applauded. Within a circle, introduce the game of Simon Says, insuring that everyone remembers the old rules.

**Script**: *This "Simon Says" is a combination of the old and the new. It is a good metaphor for doing something old in a new or different way, which often occurs at work! The old part is that the leader calls out as usual "Simon Says hands up!... Hands down!"*

*The new part is that no one is "out" of the game as a result of their putting hands down and making a "mistake!" Instead, the mistaken person shouts "OOPS!" and quickly crosses the circle to find a new place from where they can view mistakes with a fresh perspective! We will applaud their willingness to publicly admit their mistakes.* The group practices giving applause and saying OOPS to mistakes.

*Okay, let's play!* Continue to call out directions in the old way with new rules: encourage people to acknowledge their mistakes with an OOPS followed by applause and finding a new place in the circle.

(After a while, say...) *raise a hand if you haven't made a mistake yet!* (wait for hands to go up, then shout OOPS and motion for those with a raised hand to cross the circle) *Simon says you can't learn from a mistake you never make!* Continue the game.

(A good finish for those who hate to make mistakes is to say...) *Simon says Jump up!* (and then to quickly add...) *Come down! OOPS!* Everyone, including you crosses the circle, amid groans and applause! End with a discussion about mistakes.

**Variations**: Change the name of Simon to (another name) SAYS!

# 22          SECRET HANDSHAKE

**PROPS**: 0 (none)                    **SIZE**: Any (individuals)
**MOVE**: 2 (moderate / walking)    **TYPE**: Opener (S, F, E)
**AREA**: Medium                       **ORIGIN**: Karl Rohnke
**TIME**: 0-5 minutes                  **REFERENCE**: FSII-17

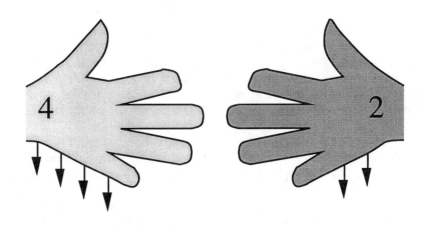

**Intent**: Meeting, greeting, and large group division.

**Action**: Folks shake hands once, twice, thrice, four, or five times.

**Highlights**: In addition to being a fun way to greet people, this is an excellent way to divide a large group into five smaller ones.

**Preparation**: Ask people to pick a secret number between 1 and 5.

**Script**: *The number you have chosen will represent the number of times you will silently shake the hand of several people you greet in this next game. If the person you greet shakes back with the same number, stick together in a group and find like minded individuals.*

*If that person shakes hands with a different number, that person is not in your group. Move on to shake with the next person. When everyone is in groups, we'll stop for some dialog. Any questions?*

**Variations**: Here are some ways to divide into different groups.

TWO:        Cross legs, arms, digits; and which one is on top?

THREE:      Eye or hand dominance (right, left, ambidextrous).

FOUR:       Hold up a number of fingers (NO thumbs or fists)!

FIVE:        Eye color (brown, blue, green, grey, other color)

SIX:         Hair color (blonde, black, brown, red, grey, bald).

SEVEN:     Day of the week you were born or do your laundry.

EIGHT:      Blood types (A+, B+, AB+, O+, A-, B-, AB-, O-).

NINE:       Shoe sizes ($\leq$ 5, 6, 7, 8, 9, 10, 11, 12, and $\geq$ 13).

TEN:         Birth dates or birth years ending in 0, 1, 2, 3,...9.

ELEVEN:     Number of kids in your family (0, 1, 2, 3,...10+).

TWELVE:     Your zodiac star sign or the month of your birthday.

# 23          CREATIVE GREETINGS

**PROPS**: 0 (none)                          **SIZE**: Any (partners)
**MOVE**: 2 (moderate / walking)    **TYPE**: Opener (S, F, E, C)
**AREA**: Medium                          **ORIGIN**: Unknown
**TIME**: 5-15 minutes                    **REFERENCE**: New

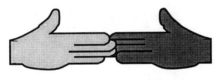

Shake Hands OR High Five!

**Intent**: Change, creativity, and learn a few names.

**Action**: People explore many creative ways of greeting each other.

**Highlights**: People sometimes prefer the comfort of impersonal handshakes or no greetings at all. Since group work is often about relationships, creative greetings affords people the chance to begin at familiar levels and gradually expand their comfort levels. The safety provided by a partnership and permission to be silly works.

**Preparation**: Ask people to find partners, shake their hand, and then learn their names and something new about them.

**Script**: *Now that you have greeted one another in a comfortable and generally acceptable manner with a handshake, we would like to explore some other ways of greeting one another. In the next 2 minutes, please greet five people with a "high-five" slap. GO!*

*Now, to expand our creativity, please greet five more people in a way that you've never greeted anyone before. For example, you might try an "elbowshake" instead of a handshake.* Demonstrate this by cupping your partner's elbow as they cup yours and shake forearms much like hands. *Remember to exchange names and when someone greets you in a new and unusual way, please greet them in return the exact same way. Any questions? GO!*

**Variations**: When people are anxious or have mixed emotions about leaving a program, using creative handshakes to say good-bye can help with the awkwardness of not knowing what to do.

# 24                    CHANGING PLACES

**PROPS**: 0 (none)             **SIZE**: Any (partners)
**MOVE**: 3 (heavy / moving)    **TYPE**: Opener (S, F, E)
**AREA**: Large                 **ORIGIN**: Unknown
**TIME**: 5-15 minutes          **REFERENCE**: New

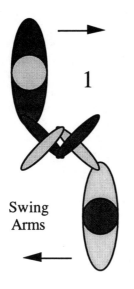

1

Swing
Arms

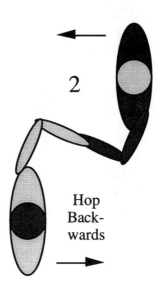

2

Hop
Back-
wards

**Intent**: Change and creativity.

**Action**: Partners seek and find alternative ways of changing places.

**Highlights**: This game provides some interesting topics worthy of debriefing discussion. Ask about changes at work and ask how this game was like or unlike change on the job. Ask about creativity at work and ask what factors help creativity or hinder it in the office.

**Preparation**: Ask people to get partners and introduce themselves.

**Script**: *Your partnership task is to change physical locations in as many different ways as you can in the next 3 minutes. No order or structure here, just be spontaneous in your leading and following. One partner thinks of a way to change places and the other follows suit, as quickly and as unselfconsciously as possible. Keep track of your number of changes by shouting out the count: 1...2...3...!*

*For example, partners could change by linking arms and swinging to trade places* (demonstrate using a person from the group). *That would be ONE! Another way might be to grab hands and trade places by hopping backwards* (demonstrate again) *TWO! There is no wrong way to do this and you have three minutes to see how many different ways you can change places. Ready, GO!*

**Variations**: Ask partners to form foursomes and exchange ideas.

# 25          CHANGE FIVE OR TEN

**PROPS**: 0 (none)              **SIZE**: Any (partners)
**MOVE**: 1 (light / standing)   **TYPE**: Opener (S, F, E)
**AREA**: Medium                 **ORIGIN**: Steve Butler
**TIME**: 5-15 minutes           **REFERENCE**: BPA-29

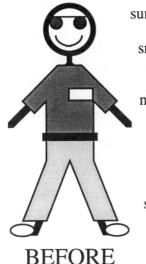

sunglasses upside down

smile becomes frown

name tag gets moved

belt gets removed

shoe goes in pocket

BEFORE                          AFTER

**Intent**: Examining assumptions about change, attention to details.

**Action**: Partners change some things about their appearance, while back to back, and turn around to discover the other's changes.

**Highlights**: This is a good exercise to punctuate how initially difficult making change can appear to be. People often learn that change doesn't necessarily mean loss: they can gain new things.

**Preparation**: Ask people to get partners and introduce themselves.

**Script**: *Take a good observant look at your partner. Notice all the finer details of their appearance. Now turn back to back and change 5 things about your appearance* (wait for them to make 5 changes).

*Turn face to face with one another and take turns identifying your partner's changes that you recognize* (allow time for their sharing).

*Now turn back to back and change 10 more things about yourselves* (this time will be more challenging so allow ample time for change).

*Once again, turn face to face and identify your partner's changes* (allow more time for discovery, then ask them to compare the two change experiences). *How easy was it to come up with the second set of changes? How was this game like making changes in your organizations?* People respond with comments about this was just like being asked to change until they could change no more.

**Variations**: Challenge the group by increasing or decreasing the number of changes according to their creativity and innovation.

# 26      QUOTES ON CARDS

**PROPS**: 1 (one only)    **SIZE**: Any (partners)
**MOVE**: 0 (none / sitting)    **TYPE**: Opener (S, F, C)
**AREA**: Medium    **ORIGIN**: Faith Evans
**TIME**: 15-30 minutes    **REFERENCE**: New

---

## A few Quotes on **FRIENDSHIP**

The better part of one's life consists of friendships. — Abraham Lincoln

The imaginary friends I had as a kid dropped me because their friends thought I didn't exist. — Aaron Machado

It destroys one's nerves to be amiable everyday to the same human being. — Benjamin Disraeli

I hate it when friends come too late to help. — Euripides

Friends may come and go, but enemies accumulate. —Thomas Jones

Friendship is like money, easier made than kept. — Samuel Butler

A friend is one who knows us, but loves us anyway. — Jerome Cummings

**Intent**: Introduce or focus thinking around a specific theme.

**Action**: Partners reflect on the meanings of selected quotes.

**Highlights**: Use this activity when the subject matter is broad and undefined. Pick general themes like: Teamwork, Integrity, Power, Commitment, Leadership, Trust, and Friendship (see opposite). A good source for many quotes is "Experiential Quotes" by T. Miner & S. Priest (available from Learning Unlimited 1-888-622-4203).

**Preparation**: Have at least five quotes per person and write these on separate index cards. Place the cards in a basket and ask people to draw one as they enter the room. Leave the basket in plain view.

**Script**: *You are probably wondering what to do with the quote you recently drew from the basket. In a moment, you'll find a partner and introduce yourselves. Read both quotes aloud to one another. Reflect on what the author meant by the words and how they might relate to the purpose of your being here today. On this chart paper or overhead projection are some questions to guide your reflection:*

- Does it have a different meaning today than when it was written?
- Is it true for your personal world and your professional world?
- If the quote were to have a more powerful meaning for you, how would you change it?

*There are no right or wrong answers here, only a dialogue between the two of you to expand your understanding of the quote. If you want to swap quotes, there are plenty more in the basket over here.*

*If, you find a quote that means something profound to you, after you discuss it, you may keep it. Simply put it in your pocket and quickly draw another one from the basket. Any questions? Work until I call STOP! You'll have about a half hour to do this.*

**Variations**: With more than a half hour to talk, encourage people to find new partners and repeat the process. Quotes may also be exchanged. Instead of partners, hold discussions in small groups. Ask people to share their favorite quotes in a debriefing session.

# 27                                    TEAM CHEER

**PROPS**: 0 (none)                    **SIZE**: 10-20
**MOVE**: 3 (heavy / moving)           **TYPE**: Opener (F, E, C)
**AREA**: Medium                       **ORIGIN**: Classic
**TIME**: 15-30 minutes                **REFERENCE**: New

**Intent**: Risk taking, celebrating, collaboration, and communication.

**Action**: Groups develop and perform a team identification cheer.

**Highlights**: This activity may be the first real emotional risk of the day and may be outside some people's comfort zone. Therefore, be particularly enthusiastic and supportive in your presentation.

**Preparation**: Give clear instructions and time limits for groups to plan and present. A demonstration of cheers can be very helpful.

**Script**: *Since we'll be working together in close groups for this program, it's a good idea to forge some individual team identities with a cheer. A team cheer can serve as a connection point, as a rallying cry, and as a reason to celebrate. Long after the program is over, team cheers remain tattooed in the kinesthetic brain and echo down office corridors or up elevator shafts.*

*Your group will have 15 minutes to create and get ready to perform your group cheer for everyone. Your cheer must have 3 elements: 1) a catchy and memorable name, 2) an accompanying sound and slogan that makes your blood run hot, and 3) a motion that spurs you into action! Your cheer should reflect the spirit of your team when it is working at its highest level of word and deed. Go for extraordinary, potent, dynamic, vigorous, wild, and unforgettable!* (use descriptors that are motivational to your particular groups). *Any questions? Take the next 15 minutes to create your cheer.*

After 15 minutes, gather the groups for their performances. As Master of Ceremonies, orchestrate loud applause after each cheer.

**Variations**: Throughout the program, celebrate the smallest (and largest) successes with rousing repeats of these cheers. Revisit their team cheers at the end the program with a round for the road! See also #91: Celebration Circles for related closing activities.

# 28                                CATEGORIES

**PROPS**: 1 (one only)          **SIZE**: 50-100
**MOVE**: 2 (moderate / walking) **TYPE**: Socializer (O, F, E)
**AREA**: Large                  **ORIGIN**: Karl Rohnke
**TIME**: 15-30 minutes          **REFERENCE**: BBA-143

## Number of years employed by this company

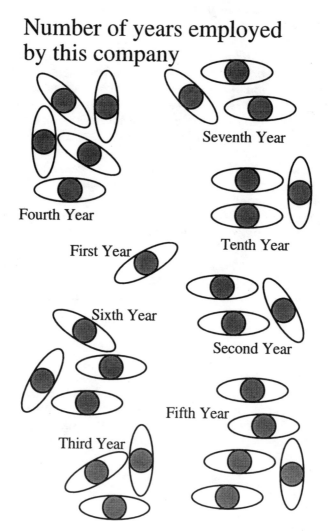

Fourth Year

Seventh Year

Tenth Year

First Year

Sixth Year

Second Year

Third Year

Fifth Year

**Intent**: Find commonalities and get to know each other better.

**Action**: People get together in common categories and then talk.

**Highlights**: This is a great activity for soon after group arrival.

**Preparation**: You may need a whistle or other attention device for noisy groups. The key to this activity is selecting categories so that everyone can participate in a group conversation.

**Script**: *This game is about incorporating yourself into a common group and having a short conversation with people you meet there. You may not finish your conversation in the time we have, but these are conversation starters, which I hope you'll pick up on later.*

*In a minute, I'll call out a category like SIBLINGS and you'll find everyone else who has the same number as you (ZERO can be a group). I might call out SOCK COLOR and you'll find the group where everyone has the same color socks (NONE can be a group)*

*Once you find a common category group start a conversation about yourselves. Start with the reason you are there ,what it was like as an only child, or why you choose not to wear socks. Find other things you might have in common with folks and talk further.*

*In a few minutes, I'll blow the whistle. We'll see who is in which groups and then we'll try another category. Any questions? GO!*

**Variations**: Ask people for their category ideas. Here are some suggestions (remember "none" and "don't know" can be a group).

WEARING: the same jewelry, type of shoes, color of pants / shirt.
HAVING: the same hair style / length, or color of eyes / hair / nails.
OWNING: the same kind of pet, car, computer, cell phone, pager.
NUMBER: of bedrooms / toilets in your home, kids in your family.
TIME OF DAY: that you exercise, shower / bathe, read the paper.
FAVORITE: type of food, drink, books, movies, music, exercise.

# 29                    INCORPORATIONS

**PROPS**: 1 (one only)          **SIZE**: Any (partners)
**MOVE**: 1 (light / standing)   **TYPE**: Socializer (O, F)
**AREA**: Medium                 **ORIGIN**: Classic
**TIME**: 15-30 minutes          **REFERENCE**: New

## WHAT IS YOUR FAVORITE PASTTIME?

I enjoy fishing!                 I really like golf!

I recently took a trip           I've been taking
to Lake Taupo in                 lessons locally in
New Zealand for                  order to improve
some of the best                 my handicap, but
fishing in the world.            recently I've had
I can't wait until...            trouble with my...

**Intent**: Find commonalities and get to know one another better.

**Action**: Partners get together and answer facilitator questions.

**Highlights**: This is a great activity for after immediate arrival.

**Preparation**: You may need a whistle for large noisy groups.

**Script**: *In this game, find a partner and have a discussion about a topic I'll provide. You may not finish your chat in the time we have, but I hope you'll continue conversations at a later time.*

*In a minute, I'll call out a question like "HOW LONG HAVE YOU WORKED FOR THIS COMPANY?" or "WHAT DOES YOUR JOB INVOLVE?" Take a few minutes to discuss this between you.*

*After a while, I'll blow my whistle and you'll instantly find another partner and I'll provide the next topic. If you are without a partner, simply raise your hand, and connect yourselves with other people who have their hands in the air. Any questions? GO!*

**Variations**: Ask the group for some good questions or topics. Here are some more you might consider asking.

• What you would do with the money if you won a lottery?

• What is your fantasy vacation spot if money were no object?

• What is the most fun you've had lately?

• What is something that most people don't know about you?

• What is the greatest challenge you face at work?

• What gives you the most joy in your job?

• What is something you want to change in the office?

• If you could give one piece of advice to (youth, the CEO, your direct reports, boss, etc.), what would that advice be?

# 30                    SPECIAL PEOPLE

**PROPS**: 0 (none)                **SIZE**: Any (small groups)
**MOVE**: 0 (none / sitting)       **TYPE**: Socializer (O, F)
**AREA**: Medium                   **ORIGIN**: Unknown
**TIME**: 5-15 minutes             **REFERENCE**: New

*QUIRK LIST*

1. _____

2. _____

3. _____

4. _____

5. _____

6. _____

**Intent**: Discover we all do some things differently.

**Action**: Small groups share unusual things they do or need.

**Highlights**: People are sometimes reluctant about sharing their eccentricities or peculiarities. The result of this exercise is that most people find that they are more alike than they initially thought.

**Preparation**: Think of your own idiosyncrasies for examples. Set the tone that this is an exercise to discover interesting facts and commonalities about each other, not ammunition to tease or ridicule.

**Script**: *We all have them. We've all seen them in others. They are those unique beliefs or behaviors that a person has that sets them apart. Some people call them Quirks! For example, my college roommate could not sleep at night unless the room was completely dark. He put covers on the window, a towel under the door to the hall and made me turn my digital clock on its face to block the light.*

*Please divide into groups of 3 or 4 people and discuss these kinds of behaviors and beliefs. Your goal, at the end of ten minutes, is to deliver a short list of quirks or idiosyncrasies that your group has. We are not necessarily looking for exclusive quirks, so it's okay to duplicate and share the same quirks with others. After ten minutes, I'll ask each group to share one interesting example.*

**Variations**: Narrow the playing field to quirks related to work. Allow people to pass and/or talk about their "friend's" quirks with permission. Debrief: if we all share the same one, can it be a quirk?

Human Treasure Hunt gives everyone a sheet of paper with a list of eccentricities or peculiarities and then asks people to find others who have these idiosyncrasies by asking one another questions. For example, it is like gathering signatures from people who...

...currently own a boat or water craft;
...have trained for a triathalon; and
...drove or moved across the country.

# 31    THREE THINGS IN COMMON

**PROPS**: 0 (none)
**MOVE**: 1 (light / standing)
**AREA**: Medium
**TIME**: 5-15 minutes

**SIZE**: Any (partners)
**TYPE**: Socializer (O, F)
**ORIGIN**: Unknown
**REFERENCE**: FSIV-36

1) have been married twice;
2) own a big old dog; and
3) play golf once a week

**Intent**: Share commonalities and get to know one another better.

**Action**: Partners find three unusual things they have in common.

**Highlights**: This game works well as people first arrive. They are looking for the familiar and the comfortable. An unexpected side benefit of their conversations is that finding out things they don't have in common can still lead to learning lots about one another.

**Preparation**: Ask people to get partners and introduce themselves.

**Script**: *The word "community" springs from the word "common" and the goal of this game is to create a feeling of community by discovering commonalities. In the next three minutes, find three things that you and your partner have in common and that you don't already know or can't tell by looking. For example, working for the same company and wearing glasses DON'T count! After three minutes, be ready to volunteer commonalities. Any questions?*

**Variations**: With groups who already know each other, invite them to discover their most unique or extraordinary commonality. Challenge the entire group to find a commonality among everyone.

<u>Stand and Be Recognized</u> is a version where anyone can identify a trait and ask those who share it to stand and be recognized (it is also a non-active version of #35: Have You Ever?). For example, stand and be recognized, if you....

...drove more than an hour to get here;
...work in customer relations; or
...coach a youth group or sports team.

# 32    WORK, REST, AND PLAY

**PROPS**: 2 (two or more)
**MOVE**: 0 (none / sitting)
**AREA**: Small
**TIME**: 15-30 minutes

**SIZE**: 1-10
**TYPE**: Socializer (O, F)
**ORIGIN**: Sam Sikes
**REFERENCE**: EM-202

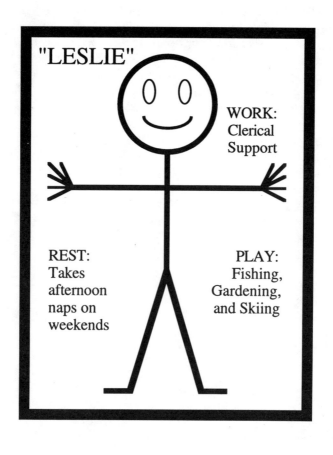

**Intent**: Find commonalities and learn more about one another.

**Action**: Groups synthesize imaginary representations of everyone.

**Highlights**: In this game, a group actually introduces an invisible "group member" who is a composite of their work, rest, and play.

**Preparation**: Have pen and paper or flip chart and markers to use.

**Script**: *When we start, you'll be working in small groups of 3 or 4 and discovering the things you have in common about your work, rest, and play habits. Instead of just reporting these commonalities, we'd like you to create and then introduce a new "group member" who has a combination of the actual work, rest, and play attributes of the folks in your small group. Don't forget to name this person!*

*Before you present your imaginary friend, please draw him or her with pen and paper or the markers and flip charts we have available.*

*If a person had the combination of the skills you have in your small group, what would he or she do for work? What would his or her sleeping patterns be like? What would he or she enjoy doing during his or her leisure time? Be creative! You have ten minutes to draw your person and then up to 2 minutes to introduce your person. Any questions? GO!*

**Variations**: Instead of asking for a real composite, ask groups for a person who would lead the ideal fantasy life that they may desire.

Sometimes people have a hard time combining their real experience and deciding what type of job or fun this "person" might have. If needed, encourage them to make up new occupations or hobbies.

# 33                    PERSONAL PRESS

**PROPS**: 1 (one only)          **SIZE**: Any (partners)
**MOVE**: 1 (light / standing)   **TYPE**: Socializer (O, F, E)
**AREA**: Medium                 **ORIGIN**: Chris Cavert
**TIME**: 5-15 minutes           **REFERENCE**: UYN-50

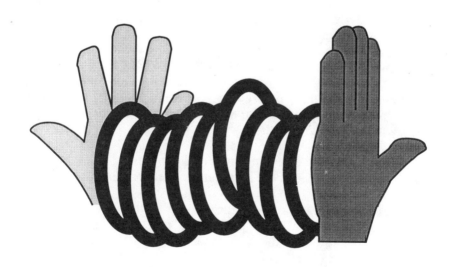

**Intent**: Getting to know your partner and working under pressure.

**Action**: Partners press together and hold a horizontal column of the most objects possible while sharing personal information.

**Highlights**: Best done as collaborative challenge, not competition.

**Preparation**: This activity works well with 4" diameter Ethafoam "noodles." These are the children's swimming and floating toys.

Use a serrated bread knife to cut the noodles into 1.25" thick slices (or order precut ones from Learning Unlimited 1-888-622-4203). Alternatively, you can substitute other objects at your discretion such as books, blocks of wood, fleece balls, or rolls of toilet paper. You will need approximately 30 noodle slices for each partnership.

**Script**: *In this game, your task is to press as many of these pieces together as you can* (hold up a noodle slice or other suitable object).

*Use one hand as a press and the other to add pieces. Start by putting your "press" hand palm to palm with your partner's "press" hand. Then, using your free hands, take turns adding one piece at a time between your two pressed hands. Each time a piece is added, the person adding it shares something personal. Once each piece is placed, it cannot be repositioned. Count as you go, because if you drop them your pieces will get mixed up with all the other free ones in the area, and you won't have known the total. Any questions?*

**Variations**: When the bridge of noodles collapses, ask people to find new partners and go another round.

# 34                     REPORTERS

**PROPS**: 2 (two or more)      **SIZE**: Any (individuals)
**MOVE**: 2 (moderate / walking)   **TYPE**: Socializer (O, F)
**AREA**: Medium                **ORIGIN**: Classic
**TIME**: 15-30 minutes         **REFERENCE**: New

SO TELL ME ABOUT A
SURVIVAL SITUATION
THAT YOU'VE BEEN IN

I took a course in the military
that taught you how to build
fires and shelters, and how to
find food and water.  One time,
we were dropped off in a real...

**Intent**: Get to know a little something about four other people.

**Action**: People interview one another about unusual occurrences.

**Highlights**: A classic game used to gather signatures of people who had done certain things in their lives. Unfortunately, all one ended up with was a page of signatures, without really getting to know folks. This game goes further by asking for the whole story.

**Preparation**: Have a piece of paper and pen/pencil for each person and write four questions on a flip chart or projection sheet. FIND AND INTERVIEW (be ready to report back on) SOMEONE WHO:

• has embarrassed themselves in public;
• was born or raised outside this country;
• can imitate someone famous (they must do it); OR
• keeps something unique in their garage / attic / basement.

**Script**: *Today, you are going to interview four different people and get the short story from one person for each of these four headlines* (indicate the list). *You have about 15 minutes. Any questions?*

(After fifteen minutes), *let's gather in a circle and hear from a few reporters. Who wants to go first?* Stories are shared and you get people to explain or share more. *And finally, before we finish, is there anyone who has anything they want to tell us that we missed?*

**Variations**: Here are a few more substitute interview questions.

• held a very unusual first paid job;
• has ever been arrested or spent a night in jail;
• can sing a TV commercial jingle (they must do it); OR
• was bitten by a wild animal (or a pet).

AND

• helped an animal give birth;
• can hum a Broadway tune (they must do it);
• has parachuted / hang glided / paraglided; OR
• was able to break a record of some kind.

# 35                      HAVE YOU EVER...?

**PROPS**: 1 (one only)          **SIZE**: 20-50
**MOVE**: 2 (moderate / walking)  **TYPE**: Socializer (O, F, E)
**AREA**: Medium                 **ORIGIN**: Karl Rohnke
**TIME**: 5-15 minutes           **REFERENCE**: BBA-127

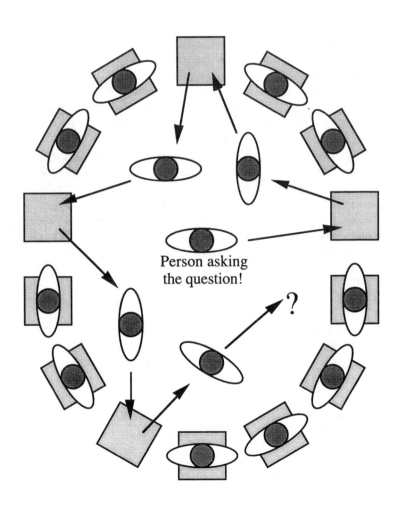

Person asking
the question!

**Intent**: Learn about one another and find things in common.

**Action**: People with the same experiences swap places in a circle.

**Highlights**: Take care that no one gets hurt rushing to swap places. Encourage people to shuffle or move in slow motion.

**Preparation**: With the group's help, create a circle of chairs (or carpet squares) with each person sitting in a chair (or standing on a square) and you standing in the middle without a chair (or square).

**Script**: *In this activity, the person in the middle will complete a HAVE YOU EVER sentence with a question that is TRUE for him or her. If it is also true for you, leave your position and find an empty one that was vacated by someone else who answered YES to the question. For example, if I asked "have you ever flown in an airplane;" then anyone who has, would change places.*

*Meanwhile, I will have grabbed one of the first empty spaces and the person who is unable to find an empty space, will become the next questioner in the middle. Now although the consequence of being last to find an open space is pretty minor, some people will still want to race, rush, and push each other. So, let's resist that competitive temptation, shuffle between places, and avoid physical contact. Any questions? HAVE YOU EVER....*

* *capsized a canoe in whitewater?*
* *been to a play in New York?*
* *flown in a helicopter?*
* *watched TV for more than 8 hours in one day?*
* *spilled hot coffee on yourself?*

**Variations**: Play have you <u>N</u>ever by changing the descriptions to the things people have not done in their lives.

# 36                                    WALLETS

**PROPS**: 1 (one only)          **SIZE**: 1-10
**MOVE**: 1 (light / standing)   **TYPE**: Socializer (O, F)
**AREA**: Small                  **ORIGIN**: Karl Rohnke
**TIME**: 5-15 minutes           **REFERENCE**: FSII-29

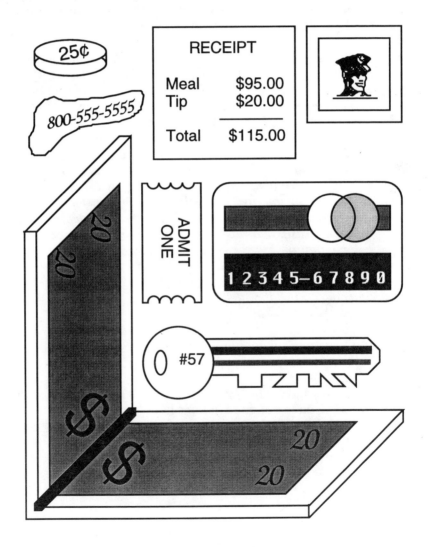

**Intent**: Get to know one another through personal memorabilia.

**Action**: People share things about themselves from their wallets.

**Highlights**: Wallets is a good way to determine the level of trust, openness, support, and willingness to take risks in the group.

**Preparation**: In advance, check your own wallet for something that you will share with everyone. Your own enthusiasm and depth of sharing will set the tone for others to follow. Go first!

**Script**: *I was cleaning out my wallet this morning and I found this receipt* (hold it up all to see). *This receipt means a great deal to me, because its from a dinner I had with my old college roommate who I hadn't seen in over 25 years...* Continue, then finish the story.

*Small things often say a lot, as in the case of things one finds in a wallet. Today, we may learn some big things about each other and ourselves, so let's start with something small. Please look inside your wallet and find something you would be willing to share with others. Pick something that tells a story and tells us something about you: something we might not know otherwise; perhaps something you value or use all the time. It could be a photo, coin or trinket; maybe even something you forgot you had.*

*Now, get into small groups of about five people to share and take turns telling your stories about what you found in your wallet.*

**Variations**: If someone doesn't have a wallet with them, invite them to share something from their purse, briefcase, pockets, and clothes or jewelry on their person. On the other hand, ask them to share something they MIGHT have had in their wallet (or other substitute) had they known they would be asked to play this game.

Penny for Your Thoughts. Ask people to pull a penny out of their pocket (or let them pick one from your jar) and note the year of the minting. Ask them to recall for the group something significant that happened in their lives (or for their family) during that same year.

# 37    WHERE IN THE WORLD?

**PROPS**: 0 (none)              **SIZE**: Any (individuals)
**MOVE**: 1 (light / standing)   **TYPE**: Socializer (O, F, E)
**AREA**: Large                  **ORIGIN**: Simon Priest
**TIME**: 5-15 minutes           **REFERENCE**: FSIII-16

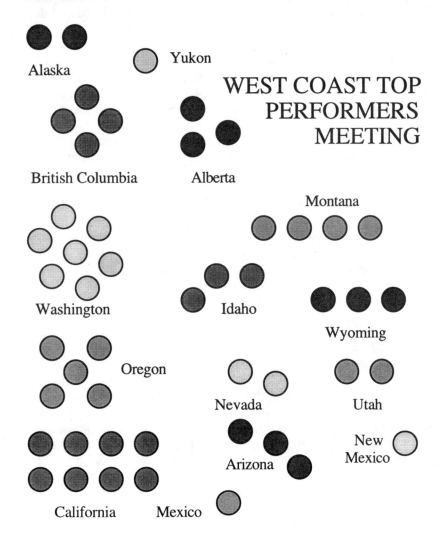

WEST COAST TOP
PERFORMERS
MEETING

**Intent**: Find some commonalities and get conversations started.

**Action**: People go to a map location that best suits their interests.

**Highlights**: You will need to describe the map to get them going.

**Preparation**: The boundaries of the map you choose will guide people's thinking. So select the region to suit the question and the audience or group you are working with. Sometimes a map of the solar system or universe can provide some interesting responses.

**Script**: *Laid out in this space is a map of the world (country / city). This way is North, which would make the other directions South, East, and West* (indicate relative directions). *In a moment, I'll call out a statement and your job is to go to that place in the world that makes the statement true for you. When you get there, you'll find some other folks with similar interests. I'd like you to meet and greet them, and then have a conversation about those mutual interests. Any questions?*

• *Where in the world were you born?*

*Go to your birthplace!* Allow plenty of time between questions for people to chat. Before your next question, go around and ask the groups where they are. *Where in the world are you folks gathered?*

• *Where in the world would you like to vacation?*
• *Where in the world would you go for an adventure ?*
• *Where in the world would you least like to get stranded?*

**Variations**: Let people make up their own questions. Vary the map boundaries according to the regionality of these questions.

CITY: This is our program venue. Where in the city is your hotel?
STATE: Our state conference is in the capital. Where do you live?
COUNTRY: National headquarters are here. Where is your office?

# 38          DYNAMIC ORG. CHART

**PROPS**: 0 (none)                    **SIZE**: 10-20
**MOVE**: 2 (moderate / walking)      **TYPE**: Socializer (O, F, E)
**AREA**: Medium                       **ORIGIN**: Classic
**TIME**: 5-15 minutes                 **REFERENCE**: New

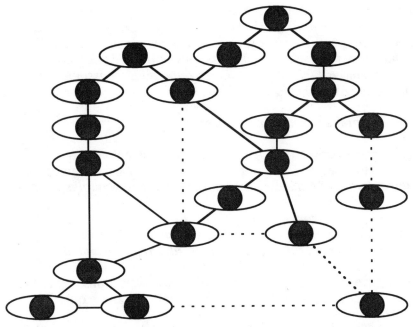

Get close to the people that you work most closely with.
Get close to the people that you work most often with.
Get close to the people that work in the same area as you.

**Intent**: Visually clarify reporting relationships within a group.

**Action**: People find their places within the company structures.

**Highlights**: This is a good diagnostic tool to determine formal and informal reporting relationships among coworkers. At first, the game may appear risky to some who are initially confused by your request. However, this is the point of doing the activity: it creates some clarity and identifies unclear, overt, and covert relationships.

**Preparation**: Clearly define for yourself what type of structure you want the group to create. Are you interested informal reporting or informal relationships? Be ready for some confusion around this and have the instructions written down on paper (see opposite).

**Script**: *We have good company cross section here with us today. I'm going to ask you to use a little imagination and creativity to fulfill a request. I want you to think about all the people here with whom you work. Consider how closely you work together, how often you interact, and in what areas you relate to each other. Also consider who is not here that significantly represents your business.*

*Now I want you to stand and move into position to form a picture of this group's working relationships within the company. Any questions? You have ten minutes to do your best and then we'll discuss why people are moving or standing in particular locations.*

Over the next ten minutes, a leader usually emerges to direct traffic and situate people with respect to who they work with most closely, most often, and in similar areas. *TIME! Okay, let's take a look at who is where and why.* Debrief their structure.

**Variations**: For the purpose of addressing conflict, you can ask people to connect on the basis of who they agree or disagree with for a particularly controversial issue at work.

# 39                    WHEN I GROW UP...

**PROPS**: 2 (two or more)          **SIZE**: Any (partners)
**MOVE**: 0 (none / sitting)          **TYPE**: Socializer (O, F)
**AREA**: Medium                    **ORIGIN**: Classic
**TIME**: 15-30 minutes          **REFERENCE**: PF-86

WHAT DID YOU WANT TO
BE WHEN YOU GREW UP?

I guess early on, I was keen to be a
physician. My parents were doctors
and they put a lot of pressure on me
to do the same. I even took pre-med
classes and graduated in Biochem. I
decided not to continue when I saw...

**Intent**: Get to know some peoples' past backgrounds and goals.

**Action**: Partner's talk to one another about past life dreams.

**Highlights**: This game can be powerful for those people who have never taken inventory of their life dreams and is a good segue into goal setting, mission, and vision. Focus the partner conversations positively. This activity is not intended to produce guilt or remorse.

**Preparation**: Ask people to get partners and introduce themselves. Sitting in chairs and recording with paper and pen/pencil are useful.

**Script**: *In this activity, your partner and you will take turns sharing information from the past. When it is your turn, you will have five minutes to speak, while your partner listens and refrains from talking. In the second round, you'll switch roles and your partner will share, while you listen.*

*I am going to ask each of you to journey back in your memory to your childhood. Specifically, I want you to recall two things:*

*• What type of career did you want when you were a kid?*
*• What did you do to make it happen or to try it out?*

*For example, if I wanted to be a firefighter as a kid, I would tell my partner about wanting to be a firefighter and anything that I did to help realize that goal. Maybe I visited the fire station, or talked to a firefighter, or set fires and put them out! Feel free to talk about more than one dream or type of job. Any questions?*

After five minutes, call for partners to switch roles; and after five more minutes, gather them together for a discussion. *I'm curious to hear some of the stories you remembered from the past. Would anyone be willing to share the story you heard with the rest of us?*

**Variations**: Ask partners to discuss any previous or early jobs they had while growing up, and/or how they got their current jobs.

# 40        BALLOON ANSWERS

**PROPS**: 2 (two or more)    **SIZE**: 10-20
**MOVE**: 2 (moderate / walking)    **TYPE**: Socializer (O, F, E)
**AREA**: Medium    **ORIGIN**: Michael Rehm
**TIME**: 5-15 minutes    **REFERENCE**: New

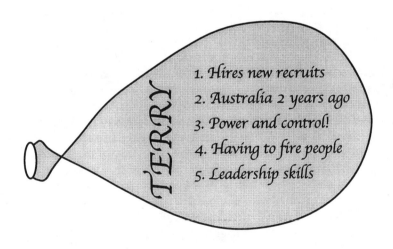

**Intent**: Meet people and get to know their interests.

**Action**: On balloons, people write answers to questions.

**Highlights**: This activity involves several juggling events where people work to keep many colored balloons in the air. Avoid high winds and sharp or dangerous objects.

**Preparation**: Distribute one balloon to each person. Ask them to inflate it and tie off the neck. Have extras ready to replace the few that burst. Give each person a broad tipped permanent marker (not pointed pen) and ask them to write their name on the balloon. Plan five questions you will ask the group later on. For example:

• What does your work involve?
• When and where was your last holiday?
• What's the best thing about your job?
• What's the worst thing about your job?
• What results would you like to see from this program?

**Script**: *Your challenge is to juggle all of these balloons in the air, without dropping or popping any. Go ahead.* (After a few minutes of fun) *okay, STOP and hold onto one balloon, not your own. In a moment, I'm going to ask a brief question. Your job is to find the person whose name is on the balloon and write on the balloon a short summary of their answer to that question. Any questions? Question #1 is....* Juggle and repeat the process for questions 2-5.

(After a final balloon juggle) *okay, STOP and hold a balloon for this last time. I'd like each of you to find and stand next to the owner of this balloon.* (Once people have done this) *now, please introduce this person using the information on their balloon that you are holding. Check with them for accuracy or clarity as you share.*

**Variations**: Having leftover balloons can present a slight problem: what to do with the leftover balloons? Save them for a later game of Balloon Frantic Foosball (see #17 of "101 Corporate Teambuilding Activities") or later in the program for game #84: Balloon Balance. Another fun way to dispose of excess balloons is Fire in the Hole. Have partners hug one another, while squeezing a balloon held between their bodies and attempting to burst it quickly.

# 41                                    SNAIL

**PROPS**: 0 (none)
**MOVE**: 2 (moderate / walking)
**AREA**: Medium
**TIME**: 5-15 minutes

**SIZE**: 10-20
**TYPE**: Socializer (O, F, E)
**ORIGIN**: Larry Rorick
**REFERENCE**: FSI-17

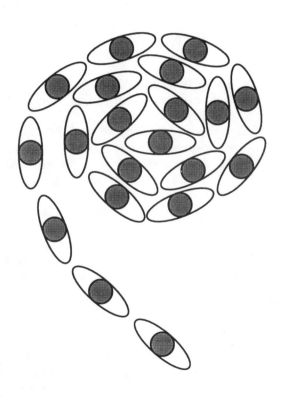

**Intent**: Establish coordination, cooperation and communication.

**Action**: Group twirls up into a tight spiral and travels in unison.

**Highlights**: Snail is an excellent segue into teamwork and trust.

**Preparation**: Explain people will be packed tightly in this game and give them the chance to pass or take a position on the outside.

**Script**: *Before we do this activity, I'd like to see us get in a line from least to most comfortable being packed into a tight group.* People get into order. *Okay, now hold hands in this new line.*

*The person at this most comfortable end is going to start twirling on the spot, still holding hands, and the line is going to wrap tightly around the center to form a closely packed snail.* Group does this.

*Okay, now that we are a snail, I'd like to see how well the snail moves without falling apart. Would you please move over here toward me without letting go of one another.* Group finds a way to move together. *Okay, let's see how the snail does with directions. Please go three feet to my left* (point), *and now six feet away from me* (point), *and lastly, nine feet to my right* (point). *Very good!*

*Now one more task. I'd like the snail to jump up so that all of its feet are off the ground at the same instance. Go ahead!* (this is the most difficult task and cannot be accomplished without cooperation and communication; eventually people will work it out). *Excellent!*

(Allow the snail to break up and then debrief to the group) *How is being that snail, like working on a team? What did you learn that may help you in this program? What will you do differently today?*

**Variations**: Ask the snail to climb over high obstacles, go up and down steps, or crawl under low obstacles without separating arms.

# 42        SHRINKING CIRCLE

**PROPS**: 0 (none)
**MOVE**: 1 (light / standing)
**AREA**: Medium
**TIME**: 0-5 minutes

**SIZE**: 20-50
**TYPE**: Socializer (O, F, E)
**ORIGIN**: Karl Rohnke
**REFERENCE**: SB-46

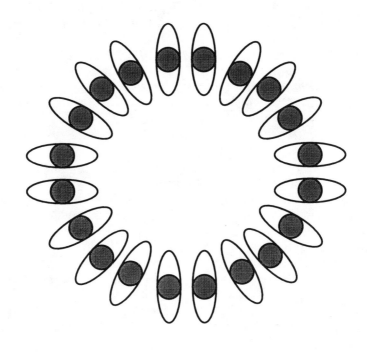

**Intent**: C cooperation, coordination, and dealing with failure.

**Action**: Circle shrinks into a single smaller tighter circle.

**Highlights**: This game can end in a lap sit, where people in the circle sit down simultaneously on the lap of the person next to them.

**Preparation**: Ask people to form a circle holding hands.

**Script**: *To begin, I'm going to squeeze one hand. When you feel an impulse in one hand, please squeeze the other hand and send this impulse around the circle. Let's see how quickly we can do this.*

*Next, please drop the hands you are holding and put your hands on the shoulders or backs (depending on the height difference) of the person on either side of you. This next game is very challenging to accomplish, so we'll need to move slowly and carefully. Without losing the circular shape and without letting go of each other, please take three giant steps into the middle to shrink our circle. Ready? 1...2...3!* People step forward and run out of space causing the circle to collapse. *Okay, let's try that again.* Repeat as needed until people figure out that they need to turn sideways to make the circle shrink properly. *Good, looks like we solved the first part of this.*

Once they have gotten into a shrunken circle by turning sideways, and provided everyone is facing in the same direction, you can then encourage a lap sit. For safety, ask people to put both hands on the waist of the person in front of them. Continue to shrink the circle until neighbors are standing with heels to toes. *On a count of three, slowly sit down on the lap of the person behind you. Carefully guide the person in front of you onto your lap. Ready? 1...2...3!*

**Variations**: An alternative to the Impulse introduction above is to send a Double Impulse (one in either direction) and to measure the time it takes for the two squeezes to race each other around the circle. Obviously, with one group, there can be no winner or loser!

An alternative to sending an impulse is Face Value, where people send facial expressions around the circle. Another is Telephone, where one sentence is whispered around the circle. In both cases, how different are the final faces or words from their originals?

# 43                    WELDED ANKLES

**PROPS**: 1 (one only)
**MOVE**: 3 (heavy / moving)
**AREA**: Medium
**TIME**: 15-30 minutes

**SIZE**: 10-20
**TYPE**: Socializer (O, F, E)
**ORIGIN**: Karl Rohnke
**REFERENCE**: BPA-98

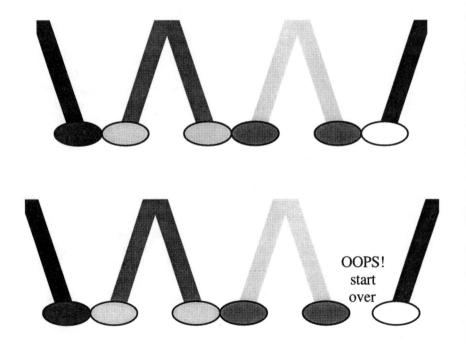

OOPS!
start
over

**Intent**: Trust, cooperation, communication, and problem solving.

**Action**: Group walks across an area while keeping feet connected.

**Highlights**: Do NOT allow feet/ankles to be tied together.

**Preparation**: Use a length of rope or masking tape to mark start and finish lines for the area to be crossed. Have people link arms and line up on one side of the marked area standing ankle to ankle.

**Script**: *Your group has fifteen minutes for everyone to cross this fifteen foot wide space without your feet becoming separated. If contact between feet should be broken, your entire group will need to return to the starting line. Any questions? GO!*

**Variations**: With several groups, encourage collaboration by inviting people from a group that has succeeded to join with some of those from a group that is starting over. Note if strategies are shared and whether help gets accepted.

Instead of crossing an open area, challenge the line of people to rotate 180 degrees to face in the opposite direction without breaking ankle contact. Alternatively, have them form a circle and rotate it 360 degrees without breaking ankle contact, so everyone returns to their original places.

All of the above challenges can be easily accomplished if people are willing to sit down and make their behinds a third point of contact!

# 44                                    MONSTER!

**PROPS**: 1 (one only)          **SIZE**: 10-20
**MOVE**: 4 (extreme / lifting)  **TYPE**: Socializer (O, F, E)
**AREA**: Large                  **ORIGIN**: Project Advent.
**TIME**: 15-30 minutes          **REFERENCE**: SB-132

ONE POSSIBLE SOLUTION

These six people stand on one foot each
and hold onto one another for support;...

...while these six people climb across
by walking on the feet of the others.

←——————————————————→

30'

**Intent**: Problem solving, cooperation, communication, and trust.

**Action**: Groups crosses an area with minimum ground contacts.

**Highlights**: This is best done with small groups. Make sure that the area is free of obstacles and has a soft landing surface for falls.

As a guideline, permit the number of simultaneous ground contacts to equal half the number of group members. Discourage any unsafe practises and carrying more than one person by any single person. Encourage people with spinal concerns or other injuries to observe, help strategize, and coach the group crossing.

**Preparation**: Use a length of rope or masking tape to mark the start and finish lines for the area to be crossed. Have people line up on one side of the marked area and give them these written rules.

- You have a total of **1 2** people in your group.
- Everyone must begin behind the starting line.
- Everyone must end behind the finishing line.
- Everyone must cross the start before anyone may cross the finish.
- In the area between, you may have only **6** simultaneous
        points of ground contact (like a foot, knee, hand, etc.).
- NO PROPS are permitted.
- Each person may "carry" no more than **1** other person.
- You must maintain contact with each other while crossing.
- Violations of ANY of these rules means you ALL start over!

**Script**: *Your task is to create an arrangement that allows you to cross this 15 foot wide open area according to the written rules you have been given* (see above). *Any questions? GO!* Sometimes people attempt to piggyback or carry one another across, even after easier solutions of hopping across while everyone remains holding hands or stepping from planted toe to planted toe are suggested.

**Variations**: For greater ease, allow more points of contact or cross a narrower distance. For more difficulty, permit fewer points of contact or cross a wider distance. Consider a reasonable time limit or ask the group to set a challenging goal for themselves.

# 45                    DIMINISHING LOAD

**PROPS**: 1 (one only)
**MOVE**: 4 (extreme / lifting)
**AREA**: Large
**TIME**: 15-30 minutes

**SIZE**: 10-20
**TYPE**: Socializer (O, F, E)
**ORIGIN**: Project Advent.
**REFERENCE**: SB-138

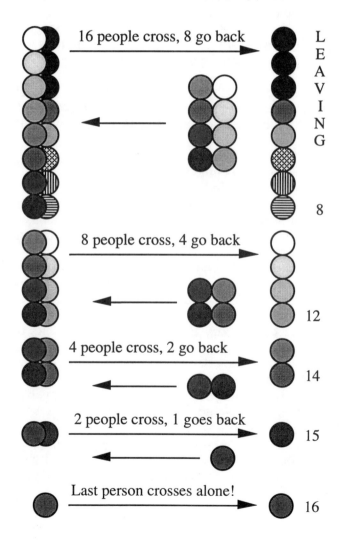

16 people cross, 8 go back

L E A V I N G

8

8 people cross, 4 go back

12

4 people cross, 2 go back

14

2 people cross, 1 goes back

15

Last person crosses alone!

16

**Intent**: Problem solving, cooperation, communication, and trust.

**Action**: Groups get everyone across an area in the fewest trips.

**Highlights**: This is best done with small groups. Make sure that the area is free of obstacles and has a soft landing surface for falls. Encourage people with spinal concerns or other injuries to observe, help strategize, and coach the multiple crossings.

**Preparation**: Use a length of rope or masking tape to mark the start and finish lines for the area to be crossed. Have people line up on one side of the marked area and give them these written rules.

- You have a total of **16** people in your group.
- Everyone must begin behind the starting line.
- Everyone must end behind the finishing line.
- You must "carry" **15** people across the area in between.
- Only people who are carried over may stay at the finish.
- All others (those who carried on the earlier trip) must return to the start, to carry again or be carried on a later trip.
- Only the **1** final person may cross without being carried.
- NO PROPS are permitted.
- Only people crossing must maintain contact with each other.
- If a carried person touches the ground, they must return.
- Violations of ANY of these rules means you ALL start over!

**Script**: *Your task is to create a sequence that uses the fewest trips to get everyone across this 15 foot wide open area according to the written rules you have been provided* (as above). *The goal is to cross in the fewest trips and NOT the fastest time. A carry over and a walk back counts as two separate trips. Any questions? GO!*

Usually people figure out their order from lightest to strongest and carry a single person over for each trip making a total of 31 trips for 16 people. However, if 8 people carry 8 over, then 8 return for 4 to carry 4, and so on; the number of trips can be reduced to 9. This may be reduced much further, if 5 people can carry 11 for example. Remember everyone must maintain constant contact inside the area.

**Variations**: If you choose to do this one for speed, guard against any possible injuries that may come from running while carrying.

# 46     SEEING THE OBVIOUS

**PROPS**: 1 (one only)
**MOVE**: 0 (none / sitting)
**AREA**: Small
**TIME**: 30-60 minutes

**SIZE**: Any (small groups)
**TYPE**: Filler (O, C)
**ORIGIN**: Unknown
**REFERENCE**: SB-102

$$\underline{\text{BUD}\blacktriangle\text{GET}} \qquad 8{:}15^{\text{OPERATOR}} \qquad \text{L\!/\!EAST}$$

**Intent**: Develop creativity, new perspectives, problem-solving.

**Action**: People work to decipher the answers to word puzzles.

**Highlights**: The 66 word puzzles (wordles) shown here are some of the best that can be easily created on a simple word processor. They can be used to emphasize many training points, especially the ability of teams to find answers faster than individuals can alone.

**Preparation**: Give everyone a copy of the wordles or project them on a screen. Be sure to give people plenty of time to solve them.

**Script**: *Let's get our brains working this morning by solving some word problems. Divide yourselves into groups of fours or fives. Each small group will work by themselves.* When everyone is ready, distribute a blank sheet and the wordles (or project these).

*Your task is to decode these word puzzles into common phrases.* (share the 6 examples above: Balanced budget, Big time operator, Last but not least, November, Growing pains, & To be or not to be) *You have 15 minutes to answer as many as you can. Please write your answers down on the blank sheet I gave you. Any questions?*

**Variations**: Here are 60 more "Wordles" (answers are at the end).

| | | | |
|---|---|---|---|
| 1. | <u>PAID</u> <br> <u>I'M</u> <br> WORKED | 15. | GESG |
| 2. | CLOSE <br> CLOSE <br> CLOSE <br> CLOSE | 16. | ISSUE  ISSUE <br> ISSUE  ISSUE <br> ISSUE  ISSUE <br> ISSUE  ISSUE <br> ISSUE  ISSUE |
| 3. | WEEKKKK | 17. | NA FISH <br> NA FISH |
| 4. | DICE <br> DICE | 18. | SUPERMAN <br> LUNCH MEAT <br> BATMAN |
| 5. | O! 144 | 19. | EILN PU |
| 6. | <u>KNEE</u> <br> LIGHT | 20. | 1935 ALONG 1975 1983 |
| 7. | T  I  M  E <br> ABDE | 21. | <u>21 LB. 18 LB.</u> <br> HAND  FOOT |
| 8. | TIMING TIM  ING | 22. | OFTEN <br> OFTEN NOT <br> OFTEN NOT |
| 9. | 10¢ <br> 10¢ | | |
| 10. | MCE <br> MCE <br> MCE | 23. | DEAL |
| 11. | 2UM <br> + <u>2UM</u> | 24. | CHOICE CHALLENGE |
| | | 25. | ALL world |
| 12. | THHAENRGE | 26. | 2TH DK |
| 13. | HIJKLMNO | 27. | CY CY |
| 14. | IE CEXCEPT | 28. | ME QUIT |

29. <u>THE WIRE</u>
    JUST

30. COLOWME

31. BJAOCKX

32. <u>  HEAD  </u>
    LHEOEVLSE

33. XQQME

34. H-O-P-E-S

35. PpOpD

36. <u>  GO  </u>
    Jan 6, Feb 3

37. BEND REVO

38. HISTORY HISTORY

39. KN
    OT

40. VVIISSIIOONN

41. TJUIMSTE

42.   √ √  √
    C O U N T E R

43. 1/4 1/4 1/4 1/4 1/4 1/4
    1/4 1/4 1/4 1/4 1/4 1/4

44. VAD ERS

45. GREENNV

46. BAN ANA

47. SIDK DKIS

48. •THAT'S

49. SIGHT LOVE
    SIGHT
    SIGHT

50. <u> GROUND </u>
    FEET FEET
    FEET FEET
    FEET FEET

51. PERFORMANCE
    PERFORMANCE

52. BALLO

53. NIRENDEZVOUSGHT

54. RUNNING SCHEDULE

55. <u>  0  </u>
    B.Sc.
    M.Ed.
    Ph.D.

56. Dr.
    DOCTOR

57.   R
    R O A D
      A
      D

58. <u>STAND</u>
    MISS

59. ECNALG

60. LOOK KOOL +ING

## ANSWERS:

1. I'm overworked & under paid
2. Foreclose (Four Close)
3. Long weekend
4. Paradise
5. Oh gross!
6. Neon light
7. Long time no see (C)
8. Split second timing
9. Paradigm shift
10. 3 blind mice (no eyes)
11. Forum
12. Hang in there
13. Water (H to O)
14. I before E except after C
15. Scrambled eggs
16. Tennis shoes
17. Tuna fish
18. Hero sandwich
19. Line up in alphabetical order
20. Along in years
21. Wait on hand and foot
22. More often than not
23. Big deal
24. Challenge by choice
25. It's a small world after all
26. Tooth decay
27. Cyclone
28. Quit following me
29. Just under the wire
30. Low income
31. Jack in the box
32. Head over heels in love
33. Excuse me
34. Dashed hopes
35. Two peas in a pod
36. Go on a double date
37. Bend over backwards
38. History repeating itself
39. Square knot
40. Double vision
41. Just in time
42. Checkout counter
43. Close quarters
44. Space invaders
45. Green with envy
46. Banana split
47. Mixed up kids
48. That's beside the point
49. Love at first sight
50. Six feet underground
51. Repeat performance
52. Absentee Ballot (no T)
53. Midnight rendezvous
54. Running ahead of schedule
55. Three degrees below zero
56. Paradox
57. Crossroads
58. Misunderstand
59. Backwards glance
60. Look both ways before crossing

# 47  PING PONG PYRAMID PUZZLE

**PROPS**: 1 (one only)          **SIZE**: Any (small groups)
**MOVE**: 0 (none / sitting)     **TYPE**: Filler (O, E, C)
**AREA**: Small                  **ORIGIN**: Classic
**TIME**: 15-30 minutes          **REFERENCE**: QS-181

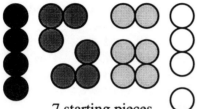
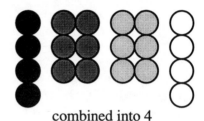

7 starting pieces          combined into 4

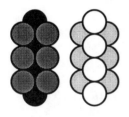
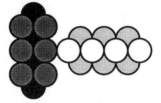
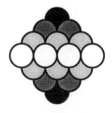

2 identical          one half rotated          finished
halves               90 degrees                pyramid

**Intent**: Provide some thinking exercises and practice with puzzles.

**Action**: Small groups assemble their pieces of a puzzle made from ping pong balls or a variety of any other puzzle collections.

**Highlights**: Also good as a problem solving team-building task.

**Preparation**: With a hot glue gun, securely glue 20 ping pong (table tennis or even golf balls) together in seven arrangements (as diagrammed above): a single ball, a pair of balls, three balls in a line, four balls in a line, four balls in a square, and three balls in an L-shape (you'll need two of these).  Have a set of 7 for each group.

**Script**: In a small group of 7 people, give everybody their own piece of the puzzle (with 14 people, have pairs share a piece). *Each person (pair) is responsible for the placement of their own piece and your task is to make a symmetrical pyramid from only these pieces.*

**Variations**: Use different sized balls to make the puzzle larger or smaller. To make the puzzle easier, combine some of the pieces to make four pieces (a pair of 1X4's and a pair of 2X3's). Instead of this puzzle, substitute any store bought or homemade puzzle. Here are alternative puzzles from Learning Unlimited 1-(888)-622-4203.

Bolt in a Bottle: a piece of wood with a bolt in it will not come out of a glass bottle until the bolt is removed. Order one or make your own from the directions on pages 28-31 of Executive Marbles.

Sam Sikes' Cross: two pieces of wood are locked together and will not come apart until the secret of unlocking is discovered. Look for instructions in Sam's next book or order one of these puzzles.

Simon Priest has developed a series of puzzles for each letter of the alphabet (A-Z) and every number (0-9). These can be used to spell out the name of your company or a particular program theme.

Puzzle Pieces

# 48 MATCHSTICKS & TOOTHPICKS

**PROPS**: 1 (one only)          **SIZE**: Any (small groups)
**MOVE**: 0 (none / sitting)      **TYPE**: Filler (O, E, C)
**AREA**: Small                   **ORIGIN**: Classic
**TIME**: 15-30 minutes           **REFERENCE**: New

| START | TASK | SOLUTION |
|:---:|:---:|:---:|
| | Position all 8 pieces (4 halves + 4 wholes) to form only 3 squares | |
| | Rearrange 3 pieces only to make only 3 squares | |
| | Only remove 5 pieces (don't move any others) to leave only 3 squares | |
| | Only remove 2 pieces (don't move any others) to leave only 2 squares | |
| | Only remove 6 pieces (don't move any others) to leave only 2 squares | |
| | Only remove 4 pieces (don't move any others) to leave only 5 squares | |
| | Only remove 8 pieces (don't move any others) to leave only 2 squares | |

**Intent**: Solve puzzles and provide some thinking exercises.

**Action**: Small groups reposition matchsticks or toothpicks to solve puzzles according to performance criteria provided by the facilitator.

**Highlights**: Also good as problem solving team-building tasks.

**Preparation**: Have an ample supply of matchsticks or toothpicks.

**Script**: Create the starting position as shown in each diagram, read or provide the written task as shown, and let each group go!

**Variations**: Here are some much trickier and tougher puzzles, but rather than matchsticks or toothpicks, do some with pen and paper. Creative groups may come up with more than the solutions shown.

| START | TASK | SOLUTION |
|:---:|:---:|:---:|

| START | TASK | SOLUTION |
|---|---|---|
| $\|\| = V\|$ | Move 1 line only to make the equation true (don't move the = sign) | $\| = V\lceil$ |

*ANSWERS: one equals the square root of one OR eleven equals eleven (in Roman numerals)*     $\|\| = X\|$

| $\|X$ | Add 1 line only to make 6 | $S\|X$ |

*ANSWERS: add a curvy line 'S' to spell SIX OR add the number 6 to give one times six = 6*     $\|X6$

| ☐☐☐ | Take away only 2 (rearrange only 5 others) to leave 2 | $\top W ☐$ |
| ☐☐☐ | Take away only 3 (rearrange only 3 others) to leave 10 | $\top E N$ |
| ☐☐☐ | Take away only 1 (rearrange only 2 others) to leave 1 | $☐ N E$ |

# 49     INTERVIEW QUESTIONS

**PROPS**: 1 (one only)
**MOVE**: 0 (none / sitting)
**AREA**: Small
**TIME**: 15-30 minutes

**SIZE**: Any (small groups)
**TYPE**: Filler (O, S, E)
**ORIGIN**: Classic
**REFERENCE**: New

## INTERVIEW QUESTIONS

1. What is at the end of infinity?

2. In Monopoly, if you started from GO and rolled a 2, a 12, and then a 2, where would you end up?

3. Approximately how many grooves are found on a vinyl record?

4. How many animals of each species did Moses take into the Ark?

5. If you have a kerosene lamp and a candle, and only one match, which do you light first?

6. A 10 foot long rope ladder hangs over the side of a boat that is anchored in a harbor. The ladder rungs are spaced 1 foot apart and the bottom rung rests on the surface of the water. If the tide rises at the rate of 9 inches per hour, how long before the first four rungs are covered by seawater?

7. A rancher had a large square field with 6 haystacks in one corner, half as many in another corner, twice as many in the other corner, and none in the last corner. During piling the hay in the center of the field, one haystack was scattered: lost to the wind. When done, how many haystacks did the rancher have?

8. Which is heavier: a pound of feathers or a pound of gold?

**Intent**: Lateral thinking, teamwork, and problem-solving.

**Action**: Small groups try to answer brain teasers within time limit.

**Highlights**: This game gets people to look at any training from a fresh perspective and works best for people who work in consistent and conservative jobs. Be ready for some interesting responses.

**Preparation**: Divide folks into groups of about 5 or 6 and provide them with a set of written "INTERVIEW QUESTIONS" (opposite).

**Script**: *Raise your hand if you have ever created a set of questions for a job interview or had to answer interview questions someone else created. I am about to distribute a short questionnaire for you to answer in teams. It will contain questions that could strike fear into the heart of any job candidate. Work quietly in your teams and write the answers on paper. You have 15 minutes. Any questions?*

**Variations**: Compare answers given in teams and by individuals.

## ANSWERS

1. The letter "Y" (infinit-Y).

2. You would be in jail (because you rolled 3 doubles in a row).

3. Two (a singular continuous groove can be found on each side).

4. Zero (It was Noah, not Moses, who had the Ark).

5. The match, of course!

6. Never, because the boat will rise and fall with the tide waters.

7. One big haystack in the middle of the field.

8. A pound of feathers weighs MORE than a pound of gold, because gold is measured in TROY weight (12 ounces = 1 pound), while feathers and other non-precious metals are measured in AVOIRDUPOIS weight (16 ounces = 1 pound).

# 50      PARTNERSHIP PROBLEMS

**PROPS**: 1 (one only)          **SIZE**: Any (partners)
**MOVE**: 0 (none / sitting)     **TYPE**: Filler (O, S, E)
**AREA**: Small                  **ORIGIN**: Classic
**TIME**: 30-60 minutes          **REFERENCE**: New

## PROBLEMS

1. A mother had a box of whole cookies to give her four children. The first received half the cookies, less one half-cookie. The second similarly received half the remaining cookies, less one half-cookie. The third also received half the cookies left, less one half-cookie. The fourth received half the last cookies, less one half-cookie. In order to do this, she never had to break or divide any cookies, but all four kids received whole cookies. If she kept two, how many cookies were in her box at the start?

2. You have two water jugs with precise volumes: 5 and 3 gallons. What do you do in order to measure out exactly 4 gallons?

3. A farmer has to cross a river by boat to reach a market with three possessions: his dog, a chicken, and a bag of grain. The boat he must use can only take the farmer and one possession at a time. If the dog and chicken, or the chicken and grain, are left without the farmer's supervision, one will eat the other. How can the farmer cross and still get all 3 possessions to market?

4. Draw a standard 8X8=64 square chessboard and place 8 coins, so that each coin is in its own square and no coin is in the same vertical column, horizontal row, or diagonal line with any other.

5. Arrange 10 coins in 5 lines of 4 coins per line.

**Intent**: Lateral thinking, teamwork, and problem-solving.

**Action**: Partners attempt to answer brain teasers within time limit.

**Highlights**: These are like "connect 9 dots with 4 lines" problems.

**Preparation**: Ask people to get partners and introduce themselves.

**Script**: *Your partnership has 45 minutes to do these five problems.*

**Variations**: Compare solutions given in teams and by individuals.

## SOLUTIONS

1. The mother started with **1 7**; and gave away **8** (17÷2 –0.5), **4** (9÷2 –0.5), **2** (5÷2 –0.5), and **1** (3÷2 –0.5) cookies to the kids.

2. Fill the 3 gallon jug and pour its water into the 5 gallon jug. Fill the 3 gallon jug again and pour as enough water into the 5 gallon jug to fill it. At this point, you will have one gallon remaining in the 3 gallon jug (5=3+2, 1=3-2). Empty the 5 gallon jug and transfer the one gallon of water from the 3 gallon jug into the 5 gallon jug. Now add three more gallons to this one to make four gallons! <u>Can you find a little known second solution?</u>

3. First, take the chicken and leave the dog and grain. Second, cross back empty. Third, bring over the dog. Fourth, take the chicken back and leave it on the other side. Fifth, return with the grain. Sixth, go back empty. Seventh, bring the chicken!

4 & 5.

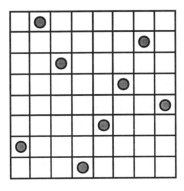
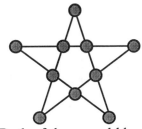

Both of these could be conducted with people substituted for the coins

# 51  MISCELLANEOUS MISLEADING

**PROPS**: 1 (one only)
**MOVE**: 1 (light / standing)
**AREA**: Small
**TIME**: 0-5 minutes

**SIZE**: 1-10
**TYPE**: Filler (O, S, E)
**ORIGIN**: Classic
**REFERENCE**: SB-53

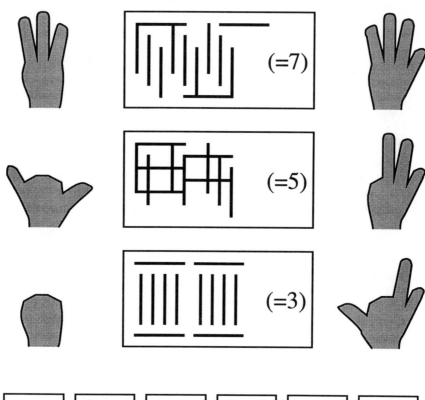

| 1 ice hole | | 1 ice hole | | 1 ice hole | |
|---|---|---|---|---|---|
| | 2 polar bears | 2 polar bears | 4 polar bears | 4 polar bears | 6 polar bears |

**Intent**: Take the blinders off, think creatively, and communicate.

**Action**: People try to "figure out the special trick" to each game.

**Highlights**: The "trick" in these cases is not to be found in the main part of the game, but in something just to the edge of it. Since people see or hear selectively, getting each trick can take sometime.

**Preparation**: Almost any prop will do, because the trick has nothing to do with the props and everything not to do with them. For argument's sake, let's use a dozen pencils for the first example.

**Script**: *Things aren't always what they seem. Take numbers for example.* Arrange the pencils in any pattern and put both palms on the ground beside the arrangement with six digits showing and say... *This is the number 6!* Rearrange the pattern, show four digits and say... *This is 4!* Rearrange the pattern again, show three digits and say...*This is the number 3!* Once more, show seven digits and ask... *What number is this?* See who says 7, continue until others have figured it out and then let them lead the game.

**Variations**: Here are some more Miscellaneous Misleadings.

Crossed or Uncrossed. In a circle, pass a couple of pencils to the person on your right. Make sure the pencils are crossed and your legs are not and then say; *These are uncrossed!* Pass two uncrossed pencils to your left and say; *These are crossed* (just like your legs)!

Polar Bears & Ice Holes. Roll at least two die (a single dice doesn't work well) and count. For even numbers, all dots are polar bears. For odd numbers, central dots are ice holes and the rest of the dots are polar bears. So 3+5=8 would be 2 ice holes and 6 polar bears!

Bugs in my Cup. *How many bugs are there in my coffee cup?* (answer 9). *How many bugs are there?* (answer 5). *How many?* (answer 2). *How many was that?* (answer 4). The answer to the number of bugs is the number of words in the question you asked.

# 52          NAME OF THE GAME

**PROPS**: 0 (none)
**MOVE**: 1 (light / standing)
**AREA**: Medium
**TIME**: 5-15 minutes

**SIZE**: Any (small groups)
**TYPE**: Filler (O, S, E)
**ORIGIN**: Classic
**REFERENCE**: BBA-44

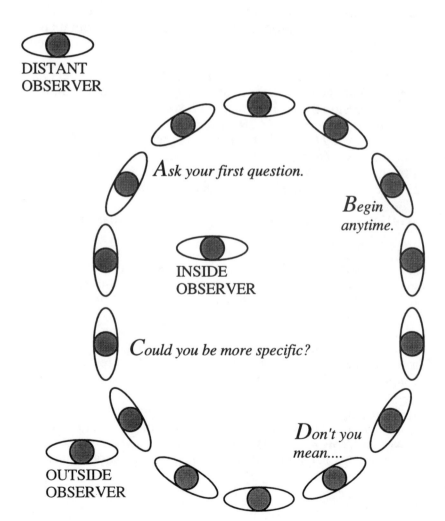

DISTANT
OBSERVER

*Ask your first question.*

*Begin anytime.*

INSIDE
OBSERVER

*Could you be more specific?*

*Don't you mean....*

OUTSIDE
OBSERVER

**Intent**: Recognize patterns, think creatively, and communicate.

**Action**: People try to "figure out the specific pattern" to each game.

**Highlights**: The "pattern" in these cases is not found in the game, but in something to the side of it. Since people are often selective about what they see or hear, finding each pattern can take a while.

**Preparation**: Ask two or three people to leave the group, while the remaining members agree on a sequence. Avoid alienating single individuals by sending a person away alone. When the sequence has been selected, ask the outside people to return to the group.

**Script**: (Speaking to the returned outsiders) *Your job is to figure out the sequence that this group is following by asking a series of questions. Ask your first question.* Outsiders ask and someone in the group responds with... *Begin asking anytime.* They ask again and another person says... *Could you be more specific?* This goes on until they discover each reply is beginning with A, B, C, etc.

**Variations**: Males and females in the group can take turns replying and can be combined with alphabetical responses. Each answer to their questions can incorporate a color or an object from the room.

Time lag. The first question is answered with a YES or a NO, and the second question is answered with whatever should have been the answer to the first question. The second answer is given to the third question, the third answer for the four question, and so on.

Number of words. Nonsensical answers have the same number of words in them as the number of words in the question asked.

Black Magic is slightly different. One person leaves the group and the remaining folks select a special object. The person returns to the group and answers YES or NO to your questions. You begin with; Is it this watch? Is it these flowers? Is it your right shoe? Is it my left earing? The returning person says NO to everything until you ask about something that is black in color and then answers YES to the very next object you pick. Make sure you brief your cohort in advance and be prepared to let others take over the roles when they think they have figured it out. Have a special signal for first pick!

# 53                GOING ON A RETREAT

**PROPS**: 0 (none)
**MOVE**: 0 (none / sitting)
**AREA**: Medium
**TIME**: 5-15 minutes

**SIZE**: Any (small groups)
**TYPE**: Filler (O, S, E)
**ORIGIN**: Classic
**REFERENCE**: BPA-63

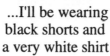

...I'll be wearing
black shorts and
a very white shirt

**Intent**: Talk about being "in the club" and being "left out!"

**Action**: People try to crack the code that gets them "into the club!"

**Highlights**: This is the classic children's game, where someone says "I'm going on a trip and taking _____!" People have to figure out what the connection is and then offer their own answer in order to also go on the trip. Careful not to alienate people with this game.

**Preparation**: Get people in a circle and pay attention to what the folks on either side of you are wearing above and below the waist.

**Script**: *I'm going on a retreat next week and you can come along if you are wearing the right clothes. I'll be wearing...* (describe the shirt of the person on your left and the pants of the person on your right). *Who else will be coming along? What will you be wearing?*

**Variations**: Here are some nonclothing alternatives.

<u>Initials</u>. Name something that has the same initials as your name.

<u>Alliteration</u>. Use two words that both start with your initial.

<u>Doublets</u>. Use a word that has a double letter like your initial.

<u>Last Letter</u>. The last letter of your name and the object are the same.

<u>Job Titles</u>. The object and your job are linked by the same initials.


And here are some really tough ones. WORDS THAT...

...<u>have silent letters</u>: Knife, Gnat, Lamb, Height, Asthma, Climb.

...<u>use all five vowels</u>: Facetious, Pneumonia, Sequoia, Airbourne.

...<u>don't contain any vowels at all</u>: Rhythm, Cwm, Try, By, My.

...<u>include letters that don't sound like they should</u>: Tough, Graph.

...<u>are foreign</u>: Faux Pas, Kindergarten, Deja Vous, Plaza, Fiesta.

# 54                                          COPY CAT

**PROPS**: 0 (none)                **SIZE**: Any (small groups)
**MOVE**: 0 (none / sitting)        **TYPE**: Filler (O, S, E)
**AREA**: Medium                   **ORIGIN**: Classic
**TIME**: 5-15 minutes             **REFERENCE**: QS-111

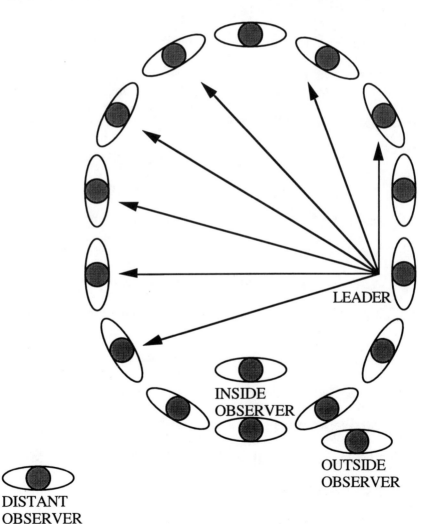

LEADER

INSIDE
OBSERVER

OUTSIDE
OBSERVER

DISTANT
OBSERVER

**Intent**: Pay attention to detail and make careful observations.

**Action**: A couple of people watch to see who is leading the pack.

**Highlights**: The group performs a rhythm led by a hidden leader who changes the rhythm, while others try to discern that leader.

**Preparation**: Ask two or three people to leave the group, while the remaining members agree on a new leader. Avoid alienating single individuals by sending a person away alone. When the new leader has been selected, ask the outside people to return to the group.

**Script**: *In this game, we have chosen one leader who will make changes that the rest of us will duplicate. Your task is to discover who our leader is. You get one guess each, without a time limit....* Begin clapping hands and watch what the chosen leader does next.

**Variations**: Pick more than one leader. Here are related games.

Everyone's a Leader. Have everybody pick their own leader and agree to duplicate what that leader does. After choices are made, ask them to close their eyes. After a few seconds, ask them to open their eyes and join in the fun as they attempt to follow the changes.

Follow the Leader. Make sure you have a beat, song, or poem to teach your group. Explain that they should follow you precisely. Just before you share it, clear your throat and then tap the beat, sing the song, or recite the poem. When they repeat you exactly, they are only correct if they clear their throats beforehand as well. The "key" can be shifting weight to another foot, changing an object to the other hand, taking a deep breath, pausing for a long time, and so on. These keys can be performed afterwards instead of beforehand.

You're Hired. *I just hired someone in this group. Who was it?* People will try to guess who you hired and (unless someone says ME! immediately) the person you will have hired will be whoever is the first person to guess, question, or utter a noise after you speak!

# 55                    MYSTERY WRITER

**PROPS**: 1 (one only)          **SIZE**: 1-10
**MOVE**: 0 (none / sitting)     **TYPE**: Filler (O, S, E, C)
**AREA**: Small                  **ORIGIN**: Classic
**TIME**: 0-5 minutes            **REFERENCE**: New

---

## *A dozen QUESTIONS*

1) What can you always find time for?

2) Never seem to find time for?

3) What is the best counsel or coaching ever given to you?

4) If you were granted any single magic power you wanted, what would it be?

5) What compliment from another do you value most?

6) If you could eat only one food forever, what would it be?

7) What are the principle differences between men and women?

8) What is hardest thing for you to say "NO" to?

9) What was the best purchase you have ever made?

10) What was your worst purchase?

11) If you had to be one age all your life, how old would you be and why?

12) What are people most influenced by?

---

Sample Questions inspired by Chat-a-chini of Learned Enterprises.

**Intent**: Sets a tone of congeniality, mystery and fun.

**Action**: People try to guess who wrote the answers to questions.

**Highlights**: This is an excellent way to bring people back from breaks on time. They seem eager to anticipate the next questions.

**Preparation**: Give everyone the printed survey opposite, along with a pen. Emphasize that the answers will be read out loud to the group. Invite them to answer the questions on the survey (include space for this), sign their name and return it to you. Collect these surveys and store them in several stacks (one stack for each break).

**Script**: After returning from break, read one question and answer from your stack, and ask... *WHO WROTE THAT ANSWER? Your job is to guess the author of this answer and provide the reasoning behind your choice. If you are correct, that person will identify himself or herself to the group.* The number of guesses can be limited or unrestricted, depending on the available time. Encourage people to be honest about their authorship. Read as many questions and answers as time allows.

**Variations**: Form two groups and ask people to write down their fantasies related to work (these will be shared aloud in the groups). Collect these and keep them separated according to the two groups. Read one aloud from the first group. If the second group can guess who wrote it, the author will join their group. Now read one aloud from the second group. If the first group can guess who wrote it, then that author will join their group.

# 56                                    THE VIRUS

**PROPS**: 2 (two or more)      **SIZE**: Any (individuals)
**MOVE**: 1 (light / standing)  **TYPE**: Filler (O, S, E, C)
**AREA**: Medium                **ORIGIN**: Mike Spiller
**TIME**: 1 hour +              **REFERENCE**: EM-180

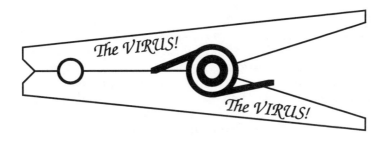

**Intent**: Avoid being the last person with the "virus" after the break.

**Action**: People try to pass a simulated "virus" around the group.

**Highlights**: Call for a "virus check" whenever you feel like it, but it is always an interesting game to visit just after breaks are finished. During a "virus check" anyone who is found to have the virus, must perform a "viral consequence" as determined by a random drawing.

**Preparation**: Make a "virus" from a clothespin. Decorate it so that it would be hard to duplicate. Keep the decoration lightweight, but bright enough to be easily seen. Write several "viral consequences" on index cards or slips of paper and place these in a hat to be drawn from later on. Be certain some of the conditions are positive to give people some hope, in case they have to draw a viral consequence.

**Script**: *We are beginning an ongoing game that we will continue until the last time we get together I have in my hand a VIRUS that I will hide on someone or their personal property. That person may find it and hide it on someone else. When I call a VIRUS CHECK whoever has the virus will draw a VIRAL CONSEQUENCE from here* (indicate the hat) *and explain to us the strange conditions they have contracted. They will then need to act upon those conditions until the next virus check or as dictated by their conditions. This person will then have the pleasure of secretly passing the virus on.*

*During a virus check, I will first ask who has the virus. If this is not immediately obvious, we will trace the passage of the virus from whoever was known to have it last. This means finding out who has had it and where it was located. Here are the viral rules:*

• *Only hide the virus on someone, if you know their name.*
• *Hide it in plain view in a public area (not inside things).*
• *No passing a virus once the virus check is officially called for.*
• *If you find it, remember where that was, and pass it on.*
• *Once you have contracted one condition you are immune
   to further ones (you cannot be caught by the Virus twice).*

**Variations**: Here is a list of potential VIRAL CONSEQUENCES.

• Run around the room 3 times and explain what your job is.

• Once a minute for the next 10 minutes, shout "Yes!"

• Do a magic trick for us immediately.

• Lead the group in singing a well-known song.

• Shake hands with anyone who speaks to you.

• Look one foot to the right of anyone who talks to you.

• When two or more people are in the room with you, you must
   maintain physical contact with one of them at all times.

• A person near to you during the virus check must serve you as
   your own personal assistant until the next virus check.

# 57                    ACQUISITION

**PROPS**: 1 (one only)          **SIZE**: Any (individuals)
**MOVE**: 2 (moderate / walking) **TYPE**: Filler (O, S, E, C)
**AREA**: Large                  **ORIGIN**: Classic
**TIME**: 15-30 minutes          **REFERENCE**: NG-123

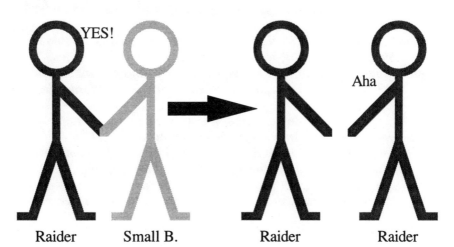

**Intent**: Systems constantly change and fear prevents involvement.

**Action**: People are frequently converted among two opposite roles.

**Highlights**: Expect noise when people meet during this game.

**Preparation**: Although blindfolds are called for, if most people are willing to keep their eyes closed, these are not needed. For safety, ask people to walk with their hands held up in front of themselves like bumpers. Mark boundaries with a length of rope or masking tape. Remove dangerous objects from within these boundaries.

**Script**: *Today's corporate market can be highly competitive and a little scary at times. Mergers, acquisitions, and divestitures often blindside people. Businesses are being taken over and being split apart on a daily basis. Here we find ourselves in that situation.*

*We will designate two roles in this activity: The Corporate Raider and the Successful Small Business. Everyone will assume the role of the successful small business to begin. You will be networking with other small businesses as you walk around without your sight.*

*As you make contact or bump into other people, briefly shake hands and say something pleasant before moving on. After a while, at least one person will be given the role of The Corporate Raider. I'll pat that person on the back and shout GO!*

*If raiders shake your hand, they will yell "YES!" and, if you are a small business, you will reply "Aha!" and be instantly turned into a raider. When two raiders meet, shake hands, and both yell YES, then they both return to being small businesses again. If two small businesses meet, they shake hands and say nothing, then move on.*

*Will the raiders take over, or will they become extinct over time?*

**Variations**: People can be permitted to make low volume beeping noise to locate one another when blindfolded. Also, this game can be conducted with sight, but it requires different covert handshakes be learned in order to indicate who is a raider and who is a small business. In this manner, the game can be continued over an entire program period in this slightly modified form of secret handshakes.

# 58                              SEEK & HIDE

**PROPS**: 0 (none)                  **SIZE**: Any (individuals)
**MOVE**: 2 (moderate / walking)     **TYPE**: Filler (O, S, E, C)
**AREA**: Large                      **ORIGIN**: Classic
**TIME**: 1 hour +                   **REFERENCE**: SB-30

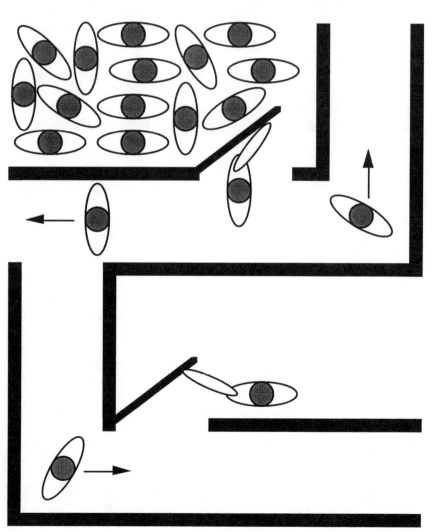

**Intent**: For fun, but also to get comfortable with close proximities.

**Action**: People crowd and cram into one hiding place like sardines.

**Highlights**: A reversal of the "hide and seek" game from when we were kids. The switch is one person hides, everyone seeks. When you find someone, you join them, and hide from the last searcher.

**Preparation**: The area used should have lots of good hiding places for large numbers of people. Outdoors in a forest and indoors in a multi-story building work well. An open field or gym work poorly.

**Script**: *I'm sure most of you played hide and seek in your younger years. In this version, the person who is picked to be IT, will hide and you will all seek out that person. When you find the IT, please do NOT announce this to the world. Instead, quietly join and hide with the IT. Eventually, we will have one last person looking for the whole group. The game is over when everyone is found.*

*If you are chosen to be IT, I would encourage you to find a very large hiding place (enough to hold us all) or, as the game continues, you'll be packed like sardines in a can! Any questions? Okay,...*

**Variations**: You can always play Hide and Seek the classic way.

# 59                    COUNTING SHAPES

**PROPS**: 1 (one only)
**MOVE**: 0 (none / sitting)
**AREA**: Small
**TIME**: 5-15 minutes

**SIZE**: Any (small groups)
**TYPE**: Filler (O, S, C)
**ORIGIN**: Classic
**REFERENCE**: QS-256

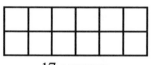

17 squares

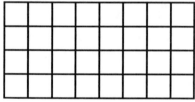

70 squares

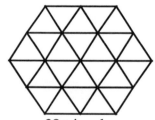

38 triangles

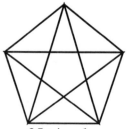

35 triangles

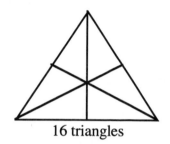

16 triangles

47 triangles

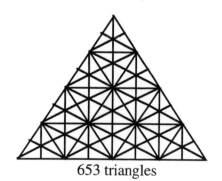

653 triangles

**Intent**: Show that many heads are better than one (or two).

**Action**: Individuals, partners, and small groups count shapes.

**Highlights**: The shapes shown have an exact number of triangles and squares hidden within them (answers shown in the diagrams). One person alone has trouble coming up with the correct answer, but teamwork can always find more than individual effort alone.

**Preparation**: Pick and choose those shapes that you would like to use, and transfer them to a sheet of paper, but obviously without the answers. Make multiple copies and give one copy to each person.

**Script**: *In this activity, you can work alone or may form groups. It would be great if we had both happening. Who wants to work alone? Okay, and who prefers to work only with a partner? Okay! So the rest of you will be getting into small groups, right? Once you are in your groups, begin to count the number of triangles and squares in the shapes on your pages. After a few minutes, we'll stop and compare answers, and see if a trend emerges.*

**Variations**: Divide this cross into 8 equally sized and identically shaped pieces, so that these 8 pieces will make 2 smaller crosses.

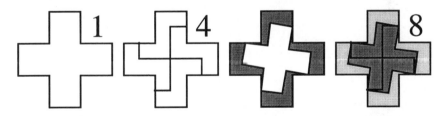

Divide this L-shaped plot of land into 4, 16, and 64 equally sized and identically shaped smaller plots (EASY: that are also L-shaped).

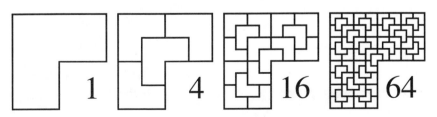

# 60                                    COUNT OFF!

**PROPS**: 0 (none)                    **SIZE**: 10-20
**MOVE**: 1 (light / standing)         **TYPE**: Energizer (O, S, F)
**AREA**: Medium                       **ORIGIN**: Classic
**TIME**: 5-15 minutes                 **REFERENCE**: SB-179

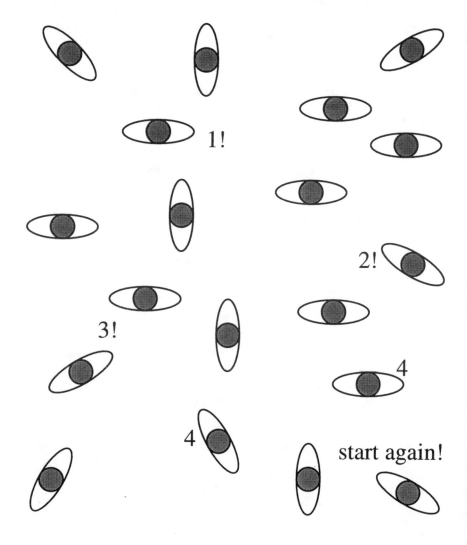

**Intent**: Coordination, cooperation, communication and trust.

**Action**: People count themselves without verbal or visual signals.

**Highlights**: This can be a very difficult task for more than twenty people, since the tendency for simultaneous responses is high.

**Preparation**: Gather the group randomly and not in a circle.

**Script**: *We'll be doing this next activity without verbal or visual cues. This means no talking, no signalling, and no directing one another. Okay?*

*We are going to discover how many people are in this group by each of us counting off a number on the way to the final total. We can only say one number once and if we duplicate anyone else's number, we will have miscounted and would begin again. For example, you say ONE, I might add TWO, and then a pair may yell THREE at the same time and then we would start over.*

*Unfortunately, there is no time for planning and we start NOW!*

**Variations**: Use letters instead of numbers. Count backwards. Count in foreign languages.

# 61                           SPEED ANIMAL

**PROPS**: 0 (none)              **SIZE**: 10-20
**MOVE**: 3 (heavy / moving)     **TYPE**: Energizer (O, S, F)
**AREA**: Medium                 **ORIGIN**: Karl Rohnke
**TIME**: 15-30 minutes          **REFERENCE**: CC-63

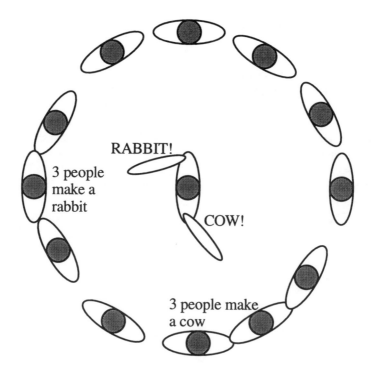

**Intent**: Coordination, speed, accuracy, confusion, and lots of fun.

**Action**: People in triads recreate animal shapes within time limits.

**Highlights**: Animals are created by the middle person and the two adjacent people in a circle. Although the middle is chosen, people on either side need to be paying just as much attention to the choice.

**Preparation**: Gather people into a circle. Demonstrate 3 animals.

RABBIT: Middle shows incisor teeth and others make floppy ears by putting an elbow with a drooping hand on the middle's shoulder.

RACCOON: Middle rubs hands together, while others make rings around middle's eyes with their circled finger and thumb.

COW: Middle holds one finger on either side of forehead as horns, while others put arms around middle and stamp feet like a bull.

FISH: Middle opens mouth like gasping for air, while others put hand to middle's cheek and wiggle fingers like gills or fins.

BIRD: Middle holds finger and thumb in front of mouth as a beak, while others stand close and hold one arm out sideways as wings.

ELEPHANT: Middle grabs nose and puts arm through loop created by this, to make trunk, while others form giant ears on either side.

GIRAFFE: Middle makes tall neck by stretching arms up in the air, while others grab middle's waist and widen stance to make 4 legs.

SHARK: Middle opens and closes "jaws" with arms extended forward, while others make triangular fin on the middle's back.

OSTRICH: Middle puts head in the sand by bending forward and putting hands behind head, while others flap wings to either side.

**Script**: *Now that you've seen how to make three animals, I'm going to stand in the center, point directly at a person, call out the name of one animal, and count to 5 as fast as I can. By the time I reach 5, anyone who is not correct in their physical depiction of that animal, will take my place in the center and begin again.* As people get comfortable with these three animals, add some more to the mix.

**Variations**: Have people make up their own animals or objects. Depicting "office personalities" can be extremely entertaining. Have multiple people in the circle center for large groups. To challenge people's improvisation, call out animals not designed or discussed yet. Add the sound of the animals for all three to express together.

# 62          WHO CONTROLS WHO?

**PROPS**: 1 (one only)          **SIZE**: Any (individuals)
**MOVE**: 3 (heavy / moving)     **TYPE**: Energizer (O, S, F)
**AREA**: Large                  **ORIGIN**: Unknown
**TIME**: 15-30 minutes          **REFERENCE**: QS-110

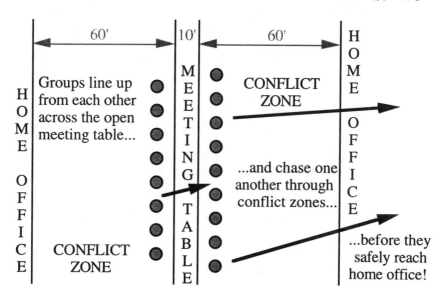

**Intent**: Get active, quick thinking, cooperation, and have fun.

**Action**: Groups present one of the above, and then chase or run.

**Highlights**: This is an update of the "rock-paper-scissors" classic. In this new corporate version, Marketing controls Finance, Finance controls Research & Development, and Research & Development controls Marketing. In a conflict, these would dominate as noted.

**Preparation**: Using four lengths of rope or rolls of masking tape create a layout as in the diagram above. Mark out two center lines 10' apart (meeting table) and two lines each about 60' away from the center lines (these are two conflict zones, with two home offices found just past the two lines). Clear the area of dangerous objects.

**Script**: *In order to play this game, we need to come up with three stances and three sounds that vividly portray these three company departments: Marketing, Finance, and Research & Development* . The group works together to create and agree on these three types.

*Now that we agree on the three representations, let's review. For example, Marketing stands tall with hands on hips and makes a deep throaty growl. Finance appears to be operating a calculator and shouts "Money!" Research & Development pours liquids from beakers to test tubes and makes a high pitched screeching noise. Let's practice these three. Okay, now form two equal sized groups.*

*In a minute, each group will go back to their home offices on the far side of the two distant lines and come to 100% consensus about which of these three you want to be. When you have reached agreement, you will come to a meeting* (on either side of the center lines). *When both groups are at the meeting table, we'll count "1, 2, 3, GO!" Then each group will perform the stances and sounds for either Marketing, Finance, or Research & Development.*

*As we all know, Marketing has power over Finance (money is only made from product sales), while Finance has power over Research & Development (allocates money for new ideas), and Research & Development has power over Marketing (creates new products for sale). So if your group is the most powerful at the table, you will chase the others through their conflict zone* (between a center line and a distant line) *in an effort to make them understand you better.*

*If you tag anyone before they reach their home office, they see your perspective more clearly and join your group. If they reach their home office, they are safe from your further influence (no tagging). Does everybody understand? Remember if there is a tie* (same two presentations), *we start over. Let's review the sounds and stances.*

**Variations**: <u>Commons</u> is a game where everyone is divided into three groups. Each group designs a motion and a sound to teach to the other groups. All three groups will need to practice each other's presentations. Instead of competing (no one presentation has power over another), the groups meet in a triangle to see if they can make their motion and sound be the same as the other two's choices. No prior communication is allowed before the groups arrive to present.

# 63         KNOWN & UNKNOWN

**PROPS**: 0 (none)              **SIZE**: Any (individuals)
**MOVE**: 2 (moderate / walking)  **TYPE**: Energizer (O, S, F)
**AREA**: Large                 **ORIGIN**: Craig Dobkin
**TIME**: 5-15 minutes          **REFERENCE**: New

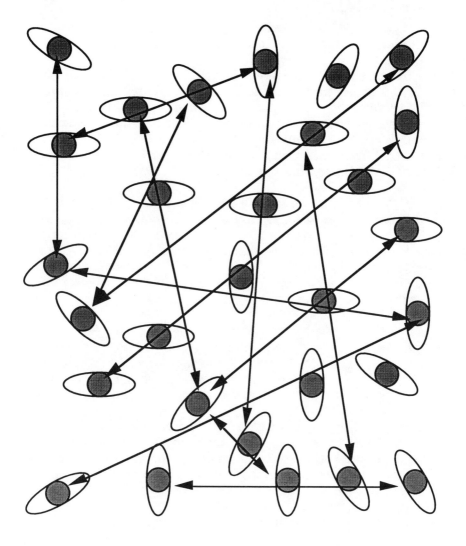

**Intent**: Address risk taking, trust, and fear of the unknown.

**Action**: People move "en mass" trying to stay aligned with others.

**Highlights**: Many people fear the unknown to varying degrees. The unknown may represent failure, loss, betrayal, being wrong, emotional discomfort, abandonment, or rejection. Simply acknowledging that the unknown is present in the room can set in motion the building of trust.

**Preparation**: Make sure the area is free of dangerous obstacles.

**Script**: *What are some things we know about today's program?* People provide a host of answers. *What are some things we don't yet know about this program?* People give a range of responses.

*Look around the group here and find a person who is unknown to you. If you know all the people here, pick the person you have known the least or for the shortest time. Don't make it obvious who you have picked. Now select, again in secret, a person whom you know really well or know better than others. These two people represent your "Known" and "Unknown" for this next activity.*

*Your job for the next three minutes is to keep the "known" person between you and the "unknown" person at all times. Ready, GO!* Absolute chaos ensues as people struggle to maintain alignments.

**Variations**: Debrief afterwards around how difficult it was to protect oneself from the unknown by using the known as your shield. Have people take a risk and identify themselves to their unknown (ask them to tell you something you don't know about them and feel free to share with them something they don't know about you).

# 64       FOREIGN EXCHANGE

**PROPS**: 2 (two or more)     **SIZE**: 20-50
**MOVE**: 2 (moderate / walking)    **TYPE**: Energizer (O, S, F)
**AREA**: Medium               **ORIGIN**: Sam Sikes
**TIME**: 5-15 minutes        **REFERENCE**: EM-48

---

### *FOREIGN EXCHANGE* Instruction Sheet

Your number   **7**   Your name   **Terry Sales**

Introduce yourself to #  **8**

Shake hands with #  **9**

Give #  **10**   a pat on the back.

Compliment #  **11**   on their shoes.

Describe how #  **12**   reminds you of Albert Einstein.

Get #  **13**   to laugh.

Introduce #  **14**   to someone else in the room.

Compare arm spans with #  **15**

Tell #  **16**   what corporation you admire the most.

Do a quick magic trick for #  **17**

Recommend a good book to #  **18**

Maintain a straight face in front of #  **19**   for 3 seconds.

Do a "high-five" with #  **20**

Explain how gravity works to #  **1**

Wink at #  **2**   when you have their attention.

**Intent**: Interaction, communication, "ice-breaking" and excitement.

**Action**: People perform several activities with others on their lists.

**Highlights**: The activities are generally intended to challenge people, but not embarrass them. Make sensitive activity choices.

**Preparation**: Give numbers to each person as they enter the room (these can be stickers for their name tags). Hand each person an instruction sheet containing customized activities like those shown opposite. Ask them to write their name and number on the sheet. Then, they write numbers in all the blanks, beginning with the next number after theirs and increasing by one from activity to activity. If they get to the total number in the group, start over at #1 again.

**Script**: *Take a pen or pencil and write your name and number on the first line of your Foreign Exchange instruction sheet. Now, number the rest of the blanks on the sheet by starting with the number after yours, and increasing by one for each blank, up to the highest number in our group and then starting to number from 1. For example, if there were 25 people in the group and I was #23, I would start with 23 then write 24 and 25, then 1, 2, 3, and so on.*

*Now that you have all the numbers on your page, find those people with those numbers and follow the instructions on the sheet. You may start anywhere on your page and try to get through all the activities in approximately ten minutes. Any questions? GO!*

**Variations**: Customize some activities to bring more than two people together for the purpose of singing a song or solving a problem. Encourage the group to come up with their own activities and assign a work related task to a random number on their sheet.

# 65      THE AUDITOR IS COMING

**PROPS**: 0 (none)
**MOVE**: 3 (heavy / moving)
**AREA**: Medium
**TIME**: 5-15 minutes

**SIZE**: 20-50
**TYPE**: Energizer (O, S, F)
**ORIGIN**: Scott Winter
**REFERENCE**: EM-32

Heave  O  Ho  All      Heave  O  Ho      All  To ge ther      Heave  O  Ho  All

**Intent**: Fun, competition, following instructions, and compliance.

**Action**: People get into groups according to one of six work tasks.

**Highlights**: Those few who don't manage to get into a group fast enough, go to "bankruptcy court" and sing a song of consequences. The song the "debtors" sing can be any tune you want, but notes from the original song are provided above for people who <u>need</u> to know.  This activity is especially useful if your program uses small groups from 2 to 5.  Simply revisit this game later on by calling out "presentation" or "cubical" for groups of 3 or 4 respectively.

**Preparation**: Clear the area of dangerous objects.  Choose a space for bankruptcy court that will accommodate the whole large group.

**Script**: *We are about to be audited by a ruthless auditor!  I'll let you know what we need to do to look our best while we endure this process.  For example, when the auditor is coming...*   (teach the 6 work tasks and allow the group plenty of time to practice each one).

THE AUDITOR IS COMING!: Stand up stiffly with your arms down by your sides and do not move (ZERO motion).

BUSY WORK: Walk around swiftly within the room and avoid making eye contact with others (stay in your own world of ONE).

GREETING: Get into groups of TWO and shake hands while saying, "Hello, Hello, Hello!"

PRESENTATION: Get into groups of THREE and put your hands on one another's shoulders, then face in the same direction to form a chorus line that kicks or walks in unison.

CUBICAL: Get into groups of FOUR and hold hands in a circle facing outwards to form a square.

LUNCH TIME: Get into groups of FIVE and interlock arms in a tight huddle and act as if you are eating food with your hands while quickly saying "Yum, Yum, Yum!"

*Okay, now that we know what our audit is based on, let me share with you that the auditor has informed me that anyone who cannot get into a correctly sized group in this game must go to bankruptcy court! If this is you, please walk over to this area* (indicate the place) *and begin singing this song. Let's practice! "Heave O Ho All, Heave O Ho, All Together, Heave O Ho All!"* (practice).

*Remember anyone in a wrongly sized group will go to court and sing the song until the end of the audit. That includes too many in a group as well as too few. If there is a dispute, you all go to court!*

*Let's review those six work tasks again. Let's sing that song one more time! Any questions? Okay, The auditor is coming....*

**Variations**: Create different groupings and movements that fit with your organization, like exercise break, water cooler, sales call, etc. For larger groups, have an assistant or two to help the debtors sing their song. Keep the action moving. Take just enough time for new debtors to be sentenced, then call out a new work task.

# 66                    STOCKS AND BONDS

**PROPS**: 2 (two or more)
**MOVE**: 3 (heavy / moving)
**AREA**: Large
**TIME**: 15-30 minutes

**SIZE**: 50-100
**TYPE**: Energizer (O, S, F)
**ORIGIN**: Unknown
**REFERENCE**: New

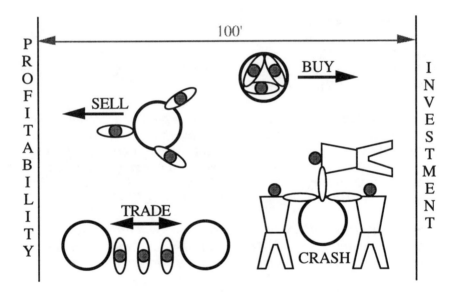

**Intent**: Respond to indicators, cooperate, communicate, have fun.

**Action**: Small groups in hula hoops shuffle across an open area.

**Highlights**: Revisit the need to SHUFFLE rather than walk or run as in the tag games from #10. Caution against tripping and falling when people get in and out of the hoops in a hurry. Count slowly.

Conflicts may surface over differences in group member's speed, agility, cooperation, alliances with cliques. Planning and strategy will be absent, since few people will agree on how to proceed. At some point, groups will begin to perform indicators with efficiency.

**Preparation**: Use two lengths of rope or rolls of masking tape to mark start and finish lines about 100' apart. Ask people to get into groups of 3 or 4 and distribute one hula hoop to each group. Use rope or webbing circles if you don't have hula hoops.

**Script**: *You are now in your trading groups with your portfolios* (indicate hoops). *In this game, you will be beginning at investment* (show start line) *and seeking to reach profitability* (cross the finish line). *Along the way fluctuations in the market will result in the need to buy, sell, or trade your portfolios and occasionally the market may crash* (explain these as per the four indicators below).

BUY: Get into your portfolio (hoop), and move quickly backwards away from profitability (the finish line) for 10 days (a 10 count).

SELL: Get out of your portfolio (hoop) and carry it quickly forward toward profitability (the finish line) for 15 days (a 15 count).

TRADE: Leave your portfolio (hoop) and exchange it for someone else's portfolio (new hoop) within the next 5 days (a 5 count). In this case, you can also form a new trading group with other people.

CRASH: Stop moving, lay down, hold on to your portfolio (hoop), and rest until the market stabilizes (when new indicators are called).

*Let's practice the market indicators again. Any questions? SELL!*

**Variations**: Play the game a second time after debriefing some of the issues noted above. Consider a whistle for large noisy groups.

# 67          GROUP CHARADES

**PROPS**: 1 (one only)
**MOVE**: 2 (moderate / walking)
**AREA**: Medium
**TIME**: 5-15 minutes

**SIZE**: 1-10
**TYPE**: Energizer (O, S, F)
**ORIGIN**: Steve Butler
**REFERENCE**: QS-114

second word

four words

first syllable

three syllables

## GROUP CHARADE CATEGORIES & SAMPLE CLUES

| FAST FOOD | OFFICE EQUIPMENT | OTHER COMPANIES |
|---|---|---|
| Cheeseburger | Color Photocopier | Starbucks |
| Side Salad | Coffee Maker | Microsoft |
| Fried Chicken | Water Cooler | Amazon.com |
| French Fries | Staple Remover | Boeing |

**Intent**: Nonverbal communication, friendly competition, and fun.

**Action**: Groups play charades with three very unusual categories.

**Highlights**: Group charades is a great nonverbal communication activity. Although any categories will do, try these three to begin.

**Preparation**: Have a list of fast foods, office equipment, and other companies; or ask people to create the clues. Write these category clues on slips of paper. Divide the group into smaller ones of 5-8.

**Script**: *We will be playing charades. The 3 categories are fast foods, office equipment, and other companies. Other than to guess answers to your groups' pantomimes, there will be NO TALKING, VOCAL NOISES, OR WRITING. Take five minutes to develop nonverbal communication strategies in your group.* Groups do this and agree on mimed language for category, words, syllables, etc.

*Please select a group representative to act out your first charade and send your individual to me. While your representative is receiving the category clue, please decide the order that group members will follow for acting out the next clues.* Provide each one of the first group representatives with a different clue written on a paper slip.

*This game resembles a relay. Once your group correctly guesses the answer to this category clue, send your second representative and so on until everyone has had a turn.* Obviously, you will need exactly enough clues for everyone. Also, ensure that each group gets the same clues, but in a different order so they don't overhear another group's answers at the same time these are being guessed.

*Once your group is finished, you can simply observe the others or offer them some assistance. Any questions? Send me your reps!*

**Variations**: Try some classic categories such as books, movies or songs. Try less common ones like pets, cartoon heroes, ice cream, occupations, dot.coms, slogans, jingles, or appliances. Let people choose the new categories. Play noncompetitively with one group.

Pictionary is a version where representatives draw clues rather than act each one out. Have plenty of paper and drawing utensils ready.

# 68                              WHO IS IT?

**PROPS**: 0 (none)
**MOVE**: 0 (none / sitting)
**AREA**: Small
**TIME**: 15-30 minutes

**SIZE**: 10-20
**TYPE**: Energizer (F)
**ORIGIN**: Adam Clark
**REFERENCE**: FSIV-8

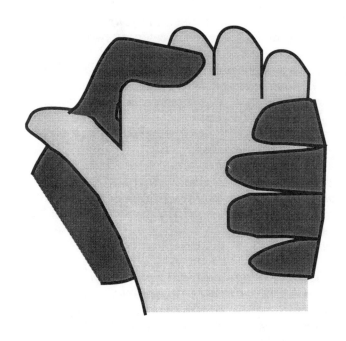

**Intent**: Attention to detail, careful observation, and risk taking.

**Action**: Before they get eliminated, people try to guess who is IT.

**Highlights**: This game is adapted from an older version, where a person in a circle, chosen as IT, winks at people to eliminate them from the circle. At the same time others try to catch the winker in the act. This newer version eliminates people with behind the back hand squeezes, so identifying IT becomes much more challenging.

**Preparation**: Ask people to sit, shoulder to shoulder, in a circle.

**Script**: *Please join hands. Place your left hand behind your lower back with your palm facing out. This means your right hand will be held behind your neighbor's back. The purpose of this game is for one person in the circle to send squeeze signals around the circle trying to eliminate people before they can correctly guess who is IT.*

*If you feel one of your hands squeezed a number of times by your neighbor, count this number, and then squeeze your other hand one less time to pass this signal on to your next neighbor. Let's try it!*

Squeeze your hand once for every member of the circle, plus at least one extra to make sure a signal goes around and comes back to you.

*Now, if you receive only one squeeze and so cannot pass the signal any further, you are "eliminated" and enjoy observing the remainder of this round, without guessing. If you are still in the game and want to take the risk of identifying who is IT, then speak up. If you are correct, the round is over, but if you are incorrect, then you become an observer and can no longer guess. If you are IT, then you can send any number of squeezes in either direction to eliminate anyone you like. No one may change the direction of the squeezes. Any questions? If you are ready, please close your eyes and I'll pick someone to be IT by lightly touching them on the back....*

**Variations**: Choose more than one person to be IT. Ask people to openly discuss who they think is IT and then a pair of people guess together, with both being eliminated for incorrect guesses.

# 69          FLASHING FINGERS

**PROPS**: 0 (none)                    **SIZE**: Any (partners)
**MOVE**: 1 (light / standing)         **TYPE**: Energizer (O, S, F)
**AREA**: Medium                       **ORIGIN**: Karl Rohnke
**TIME**: 0-5 minutes                  **REFERENCE**: BBA-48

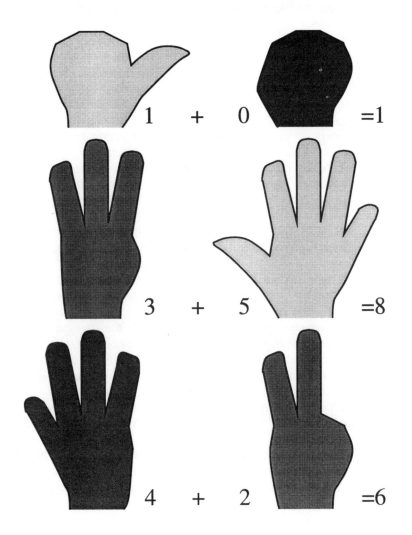

**Intent**: Speed of counting and having fun.

**Action**: Partners present a number of digits and count the total.

**Highlights**: This is a take-off on the old "odds or evens" game, where two people flashed a number of fingers to one another and used the odd or even total to decide who won or lost the deal.

**Preparation**: Ask people to get partners and introduce themselves.

**Script**: *In this game you and your partner will be showing a secret number of your fingers and thumbs to one another. Don't tell your partner how many digits you plan on presenting. Decide in advance if you will show 0 (closed fist) to 5 (open hand) or some number in between, based on how many digits are extended. When you have decided the number you will show, say "ready?" When you are both ready, call out together "set, SHOW!" and then present your digits. The first one to total both sets of digits wins. Play best two out of three and then find new partners. Any questions?*

**Variations**: Once people realize that the fastest way to total the fingers is for them to show a fist (0), all digits (5) or just one finger (1) and add this number to whatever they see from the other person, try using both hands. Alternatively, get into foursomes where one person always flashes the multiplication factor and another always offers the number to subtract. Make sure everyone agrees on the order of arithmetic operations before manipulating the mathematics.

7-11! This is a game where three people in a group attempt to show enough digits to total 7, and later 11, without talking to one another.

# 70                                 GOTCHA!

**PROPS**: 0 (none)              **SIZE**: 50-100
**MOVE**: 1 (light / standing)   **TYPE**: Energizer (O, S, F)
**AREA**: Medium                 **ORIGIN**: Mark Collard
**TIME**: 0-5 minutes            **REFERENCE**: FSII-6

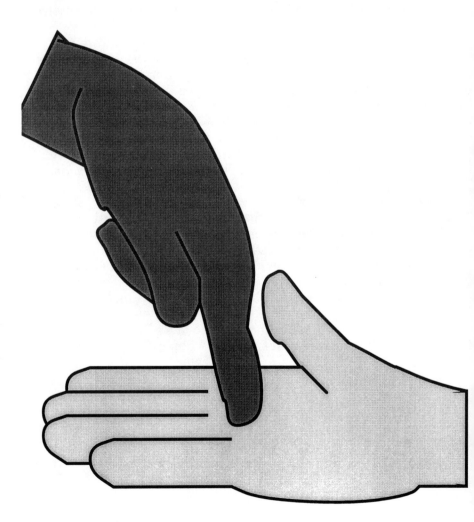

**Intent**: Speed, listening, and coordination.

**Action**: People attempt to grab their neighbor's finger with a hand.

**Highlights**: This is a good game to help people pay attention.

**Preparation**: Ask people to circle up, standing elbow width apart.

**Script**: *I'd like everyone to hold their RIGHT palm forward and up, elbow by your side, with your lower arm level and upper arm vertical. Now take your LEFT hand and extend a single digit and place it pointing down into your neighbor's extended palm. Good!*

*This is the starting positions and when I call GOTCHA, you all close your right palm and simultaneously remove your left finger from your neighbor's palm. The task is to catch a finger without yours getting caught. Any questions? Go!* (do not say gotcha yet).

Many people make their first catching attempt. *NOT when I say GO, when I say GOTCHA! Let's try that once more; please return to the starting position.*

*Okay, I'll do it correctly this time: 1...2...3...GOTCHA!*

*Return to the starting position and 1...2...3...* (very long pause) *... GOTCHA!* (much laughter).

*Return to the starting position and 1... GOTCHA!*

**Variations**: Switch hands or end when interest levels dwindle.

# 71                    CIRCLE THE CIRCLE

**PROPS**: 2 (two or more)
**MOVE**: 3 (heavy / moving)
**AREA**: Medium
**TIME**: 5-15 minutes

**SIZE**: 20-50
**TYPE**: Energizer (O, S, F)
**ORIGIN**: Classic
**REFERENCE**: SB-60

**Intent**: Flexibility, speed, coordination, playing hard, having fun.

**Action**: People pass a hoop around a circle by climbing through it.

**Highlights**: When folks see hula hoops, some are often concerned that they will have to use it in the conventional manner. Other can't be prevented from swinging it around their hips. Explain that this game uses hula hoops somewhat differently from the 1950's!

**Preparation**: Obtain a couple of large sized hula hoops. Ask the group to form a circle holding hands. Separate one pair of hands, place one hoop over one person's arm, and rejoin the pair of hands.

**Script**: *Using my watch, I'm going to time how long it takes the group to get the hula hoop to travel once around the circle without people letting go of their neighbors' hands. Any questions? GO!*

*Okay, now we'll add another hula hoop* (add a second like the first) *and this time, we'll send one hoop clockwise, while the other goes anticlockwise. The difficult bit will be getting them past each other. I'll time how long it takes for both to go once around in opposite directions and get back to their original place. Any questions? GO!*

**Variations**: Use several hula hoops for very large groups or use balloons for everyone and see how long it takes to pass several of these hula hoops or all the balloons once around the circle.

Hula Hoop Relay. Form two parallel lines of people and ask them to hold hands with the neighbor in front of and behind them. Place the hula hoop in the hand of the forward person. See which line can get the hoop into the empty hand of the back person without breaking the linked line of hands. Definitely a competitive version!

To make this more difficult, ask people to reach between their legs before grasping the hand of the neighbor behind them and to reach forward and grab their other neighbor's hand as it is passed through that neighbor's legs. Use multiple hoops and more than two lines.

# 72          QUICK CELEBRATIONS

**PROPS**: 0 (none)
**MOVE**: 2 (moderate / walking)
**AREA**: Medium
**TIME**: 0-5 minutes

**SIZE**: 1-10
**TYPE**: Energizer (O, F, C)
**ORIGIN**: Classic
**REFERENCE**: New

OOOOOOOO...

...Vation!

**Intent**: Commend, salute, and reward a job well done.

**Action**: Group displays a burst of energy as variously described.

**Highlights**: Celebration can be a valuable support for group transformations and program terminations.  They also add energy and clear the stage to move on.  The key to these quick celebrations is your clear demonstration of technique and enthusiastic attitude.

**Preparation**: Practice the celebrations and know when to use each.

**Script**: *That performance/achievement was so good, it deserves....*

A ROUND OF APPLAUSE: Clap your hands, but move them around in a clockwise or anticlockwise circular motion as you clap.

A STANDING OVATION: Stand up, bend your knees slightly and make a large 'O' with your arms downward to touch your knees. Then straighten up tall and make a large 'V' by extending your arms in the air. Simultaneously make the sounds: "OOOOO...VATION!"

A TOE CLAP: Stand with your feet about shoulder width apart. On the count of three, jump and clap your feet together, while shouting "HUH!" in your loudest voice at the same instant your toes clap.

A DOUBLE SLAP-CLAP-SNAP-YES: Slap your knees twice, clap hands twice, snap fingers twice, and shout "YES!" as you point to a person who has just impressed you.

A HAPPY SALMON: Act like you're going to shake hands, instead keep your palms flat and then pat these on each other's forearms.

A CIRCLE THUMB GRAB: Circle up standing, put your left hand in the middle with a thumb's up sign, grab the thumb of the person to your right, move your hands downward and "throw" your hands into the air (while letting go of thumbs), as the group throws out a word like "EXCELLENT!"

A GROUP BACK PAT: Circle up standing, put your hands on your neighbors' back, pause for effect, and then pat both of them.

A PARTNER PAT ON THE BACK: Approach your partners as if you are going to offer them a high five with your right hand. Miss, by going to the right of their hand, and pat your partners' backs instead. They will simultaneously mirror your moves.

**Variations**: Ask the group to create their own quick celebrations.

# 73                          RAIN MAKER

**PROPS**: 0 (none)
**MOVE**: 1 (light / standing)
**AREA**: Medium
**TIME**: 0-5 minutes

**SIZE**: 50-100
**TYPE**: Closer (O, S, F, E)
**ORIGIN**: Classic
**REFERENCE**: SB-92

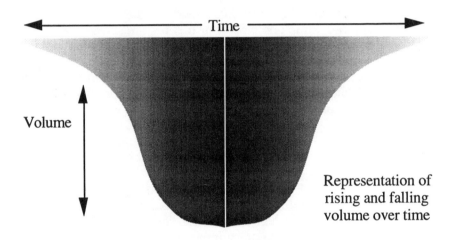

Time

Volume

Representation of rising and falling volume over time

**Intent**: Sets a tone of relaxation and a special common experience.

**Action**: Group makes coordinated sound effects to "make it rain!"

**Highlights**: You need absolute quiet for this one, it is not a good game to do when background noise is present. Focusing the group on this activity makes it a special experience. The sounds are subtle so a slow and easy transition between phases is critical.

**Preparation**: Find a quiet area and gather the group into a circle.

**Script**: *We are going to create an interesting experience using our bodies to make sounds. So we'll need quiet to start and then to stay focused and follow instructions through this activity.*

*I will stand in the middle of the circle and perform a series of sound effects with my body. When I look at you, please duplicate the sound effect that you see me doing. For example, if I am clapping, then you should clap, but randomly, not all together in a rhythm. I will rotate my glance around the circle at different speeds, so just keep doing that sound effect until I come around again with a new one. Any questions? We'll begin with SILENCE. Listen and watch carefully...*

Make the sound effect for silence as described below. Slowly rotate your glance around the circle until everyone has their arms crossed. You may have to remind some NOT to perform a sound effect until you reach them. Begin very slowly at first, moving through the eight effects listed. As the storm approaches, you can speed up the transitions. At the height of the tempest, reverse the sequence of sounds and slow down the transitions, until silence returns again.

SILENCE: cross your arms over your chest.

WIND: rub your palms together.

A FEW DROPS: randomly tap two fingers against two fingers

LIGHT RAIN: randomly snap your fingers together on both hands.

MODERATE RAIN: randomly clap your hands together.

HEAVY RAIN: randomly slap your hands on your thighs.

DOWNPOUR: stamp your feet on the floor and drum your chest.

THUNDER: voice occasional thunder noises in a deep growl.

LIGHTENING: if indoors, flash the lights on and off.

**Variations**: Remaining in a circle, people turn the same way and play these sound effects on the back of the person in front of them. Invite people to close their eyes and wait until they can feel their neighbor changing before they change. This allows you to manage the transitions and they can enjoy the feelings and sound sensations.

# 74                    CIRCLE MASSAGE

**PROPS**: 0 (none)
**MOVE**: 1 (light / standing)
**AREA**: Medium
**TIME**: 0-5 minutes

**SIZE**: 1-10
**TYPE**: Closer (S, F, E)
**ORIGIN**: Sid Simon
**REFERENCE**: PF-182

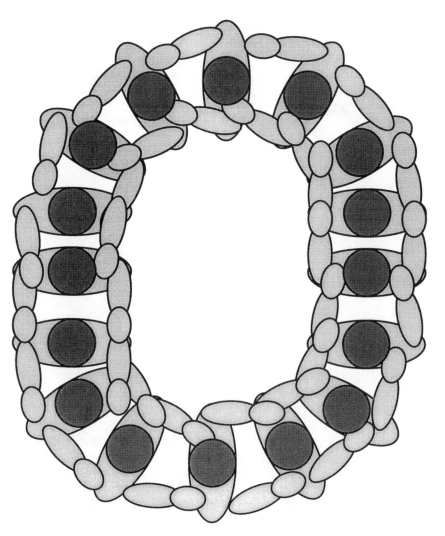

**Intent**: Relaxation, and appropriate physical touch.

**Action**: In a circle, people massage neighbor's shoulders and neck.

**Highlights**: Warming up with stretching deserves warming down with a massage. Few activities get such welcome responses from tired people toward the end of the day. Emphasize the need to be sensitive to the varying comfort levels of others. Ask for feedback.

**Preparation**: Ask people to gather in a circle and turn to their left.

**Script**: *Put your hands of on the shoulders of the person in front of you is facing away from you.* Adjust the diameter of the circle to allow a comfortable arrangement of hands and shoulders. *In a moment, I'd like you to begin massaging the neck and shoulders of this person. If you're uncomfortable with giving or receiving a massage, I would encourage you to quietly step out and observe.*

*Okay, let's begin VERY GENTLY at first. Ask people ahead what they like. Tell people behind if you need anything different. Great!*

(After a few minutes), *please thank your masseuse, turn around and return their favor!* (Spend a few more minutes at this and then), *I know this may be difficult for some, but we need to stop, face back into the center, and move on. Please thank one another.*

**Variations**: A group massage is a good way to transition into the contact version of the previous activity (Rain Maker: #73)

# 75　METAPHORIC CIRCLES

**PROPS**: 0 (none)　　　　　　**SIZE**: 10-20
**MOVE**: 1 (light / standing)　**TYPE**: Closer (F, E)
**AREA**: Medium　　　　　　　**ORIGIN**: Mary Butler
**TIME**: 5-15 minutes　　　　　**REFERENCE**: New

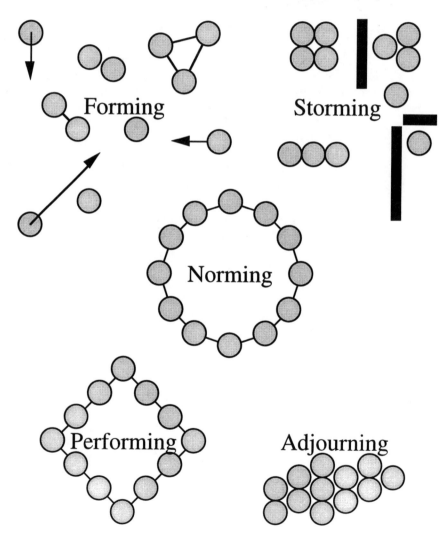

**Intent**: Show that different perspectives can become unified.

**Action**: People come together in stages that mirror their experience.

**Highlights**: This is a good closure for an intact team. It expresses their stages of development throughout the program. Since this ends in a group hug, avoid or use caution for anyone with physical concerns or personal proximity issues.

**Preparation**: Ask people to form a circle, shoulder width apart. Explain the five classic stages of group development: forming, storming, norming, performing, and adjourning (from Tuckman).

**Script**: *This circle is NOT like we were when we first arrived. In our forming stage, we came from different places with different perspectives. Please spread yourselves out to represent where you came from and what you were expecting.* Use your judgement about how much to guide their interpretations of each stage.

*Then as we focused in on the program, we became more like a circle* (motion the circle to return) *and we began getting closer and knowing more about one another. Then, we entered into the storming stage, where we worked through conflicts. Please arrange yourselves to represent the conflicts you experienced.*

*Next came the norming stage where we came to terms with how we wanted to be treated and what we wanted to do. Please get into a neat circle and happily hold hands, or present another interpretation.*

*Toward the end of the program, we moved into the performing stage, where we worked well together and supported each other. Show me what that looks like for your team by supporting one another in your tight circle or suggest another interpretation. Now as we leave today, we are adjourning ready to hug each other in appreciation and then to let go and leave.*

After each stage, discuss their arrangements in relation to that stage. At the end, debrief their interpretations of the five stages.

**Variations**: You could add a lap sit or similar performance task.

# 76    VORTEX WITH A TWIST

**PROPS**: 0 (none)
**MOVE**: 2 (moderate / walking)
**AREA**: Medium
**TIME**: 5-15 minutes

**SIZE**: 20-50
**TYPE**: Closer (S, F, E)
**ORIGIN**: Sam Sikes
**REFERENCE**: ZG-192

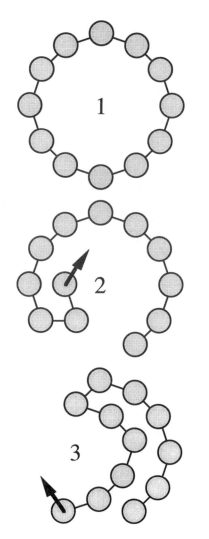

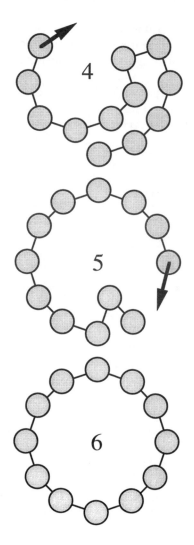

**Intent**: A reminder to take back what people have learned to others.

**Action**: Circle looks in, folds back to look out, and twists back in.

**Highlights**: When the twist occurs at the end of the activity, some people may have trouble turning without letting go of hands. If this happens,be ready to suggest that they turn in the other direction.

**Preparation**: Ask people to form a large circle holding hands.

**Script**: *In this closing, I want everyone to keep holding hands until I ask you to let go at the end. Now, we've all been looking inward during the last few days ,while we've also been learning how to be effective as a team. What are some things that we have gained by looking inward?* People share the team lessons they have learned.

*Soon, we will be traveling back to our homes and offices, but before we go, I want each of you to have an opportunity to share something positive with everyone else. I'm going to drop hands with my neighbor on the left and begin to walk right with the line following me. As I pass each person, I'll say something positive to them and they will do the same back to me. Any questions? Okay, here we go....* (fold the circle back on itself, as diagramed, and go slowly to make sure everyone gets a chance to exchange positives).

After your last exchange with the neighbor you left at the start, keep going directly around the open circle until you meet that neighbor again and then rejoin hands so that the circle is facing outwards!

*Now it is time to take what we learned or experienced here and to transfer it back to the outside world we will be returning to.*

*Lastly, let's twist around slowly, while staying connected, to look inwards one final time. What do we see?* People share their new perspectives on the program, as they stand in a smaller circle with their arms crossed in front of them, still holding hands. *Regardless of where we go next, this has brought us closer.* Let go of hands!

**Variations**: For less intensity, drop positive exchanges and weave the line under arms and through the remainder of the standing circle.

# 77    DUM DUM DADA DADA

**PROPS**: 0 (none)
**MOVE**: 0 (none / sitting)
**AREA**: Medium
**TIME**: 5-15 minutes

**SIZE**: 20-50
**TYPE**: Closer (O, S, F, E)
**ORIGIN**: Unknown
**REFERENCE**: New

Dum dum dada dada    Dum dum dadaaaa    Dum dum dada dada    Dum dum dadaaaa

Dum dum dada dada    Dum dum dada dada    Dum dum dada dada    Dum dum dum...!

**Intent**: Community building and bonding by common experience.

**Action**: Circle of people sings celebration song with movements.

**Highlights**: People tend to be anxious about singing, but they may laugh and have fun with this great way to end a successful program. This activity can be done standing, if you don't have chairs to sit in.

**Preparation**: Ask folks to form a circle of closely touching chairs. As you practice this with people go slowly at first and then speed up as they begin to learn it. Teach it in bits, then assemble the whole.

**Script**: *We are about to sing a celebration song called "Dum Dum Dada Dada!" I will sing it through the first time and then, you sing it with me after. Listen carefully to the words: they're easy to get mixed up.* Sing through the song using the music shown opposite. *Did you get it? Let's try it together!* Lead the song with the group.

*Now I said this was a celebration song. It doesn't sound much like a celebration yet, so we will add some movements to it.* Add these movements, one at a time, then sing all the verses straight through.

DOUBLE PAT: Start with hands on your knees, pat your knees twice, pat the knees of your RIGHT neighbor twice, then pat your knees twice again, and pat the knees of your LEFT neighbor twice. Repeat throughout the first verse. Pat your knees on a "dum dum" and either neighbor's knees on a "dada dada!" Go right before left.

FIRST EXCLAMATION: At the end of the first verse, yell "Woo!"

RUSSIAN DANCER: To start, hold your folded arms in front of you like a stereotypical Russian dancer. Extend both arms straight out in front of you, bend your right arm back to its starting position, then bend your left arm back to join it so both your arms are folded again, then right arm extended and left arm extended. Repeat these until you finish the second verse. Your arms should end up folded. Right before left, bend arms back on "dum" and extend on "dada!"

SECOND EXCLAMATION: Raise both arms above your head, kick out one leg and, at the end of the second verse, shout "Hey!"

NOSE AND EAR GRAB: Start by patting your knees twice, then ignore your neighbor and grab your nose with your LEFT hand and your left ear with your RIGHT hand. Pat twice again and reverse the grab position: right hand to nose and left to right ear. Repeat the movement throughout the final and most difficult verse.

FINAL EXCLAMATION: Clap hands at the end of the final verse!

**Variations**: If you choose not sing, use a tape recorder with the song on it. Then, make up your own movements to the song.

# 78                    HIDDEN FEEDBACK

**PROPS**: 1 (one only)          **SIZE**: 1-10
**MOVE**: 1 (light / standing)    **TYPE**: Closer
**AREA**: Medium                  **ORIGIN**: Mike Gass
**TIME**: 15-30 minutes          **REFERENCE**: New

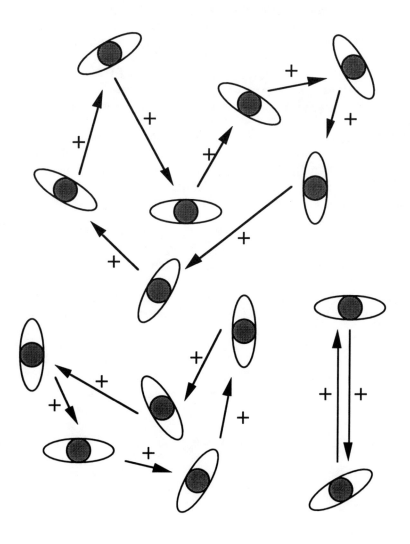

**Intent**: Giving peer feedback and appreciating personal strengths.

**Action**: People reveal who they observed and give them feedback.

**Highlights**: This is best for multiday programs where people have lots of varied opportunities to observe each other in action. During closure, the chance of emotional responses can be high, since some find receiving positive feedback can be harder than giving it. Take notes during this activity, so you can refer to them in follow-ups.

**Preparation**: Before the group has had much interaction, distribute index cards or slips of paper. Ask people to print their name on one and put it into the box you have provided. Have them draw a name from the box (returning and drawing again, if they get their own name). Explain that they are to observe the person whose name they drew and note that person's positive behaviors in the program. Encourage them to remain anonymous, but take notes if they want.

**Script**: (At the end of the program), *I hope you recall that each of you drew the name of a person to observe during the program. This is the time and place for giving those people their positive feedback. I would like you to take turns revealing who you observed and share publicly something that you were impressed by or something you saw them doing well. Here are some ground rules to help you* (have these on a flip chart or overhead projector).

* *Be specific and sincere. This is a rare opportunity for someone to receive this kind of feedback.*
* *After the observer has given positive feedback, anyone else may add their observations about that person.*
* *Most importantly, when giving feedback, say it to the person by making eye contact and using words like "you" and "I."*

*After you have received your feedback, it is then your turn to give feedback to the person that you were observing during the program. We will continue on through the group. Okay, who wants to start?*

**Variations**: Include gift giving with the feedback, such as ones that people have created with their specific recipient in mind. However, you may also consider giving everyone a manufactured memento or a natural totem as in #95: Souvenir Symbol.

# 79          GROUP PHOTOGRAPH

**PROPS**: 2 (two or more)      **SIZE**: 10-20
**MOVE**: 2 (moderate / walking)  **TYPE**: Closer (F, E)
**AREA**: Medium                **ORIGIN**: Classic
**TIME**: 15-30 minutes         **REFERENCE**: New

**Intent**: Review and capture the highlight events of the program.

**Action**: A real photo is taken as a group recreates their experience.

**Highlights**: The take-away from this activity is a real photograph. Find locations with clear backgrounds and good lighting. Use this as a way for the group to revisit significant program memories.

**Preparation**: Have one or more cameras ready to record the group presentation. Have plenty of "props" (program equipment, arts and craft supplies) for the group to use in recreating their presentation.

**Script**: *Throughout this program, you have been working on your goals as a team in a wide variety of ways. You may have thought many of the experiences you had are gone forever. In fact, I want you to recapture your best interpretations of the most significant moments from the past few days. I have a camera here and I'll be taking still photographs of your presentations. You'll get copies!*

*Please spend 20 minutes getting ready. You can work in small groups or as a whole. Be sure to include any props necessary to convey meaning to someone who was not present at the event. Any questions?*

**Variations**: Create photographic themes like the funniest moment, most challenging task, key breakthrough opportunity, and greatest lesson learned. Use video cameras to film the preparations.

Alternatively, people can plan and present dramatic <u>Skits</u>. This one can take a long time for groups to plan, unless you are very specific about wanting a SHORT skit and NOT a multi-act play! You may wish to use a video camera to record the skits and their planning.

# 80

# CAPTIONS

**PROPS**: 0 (none)
**MOVE**: 1 (light / standing)
**AREA**: Medium
**TIME**: 5-15 minutes

**SIZE**: 10-20
**TYPE**: Closer (F, E)
**ORIGIN**: Unknown
**REFERENCE**: New

# ONE FOR ALL and ALL FOR ONE!

**Intent**: Remember and share a pictureworthy moment in time.

**Action**: Circle shares memories through captions of snapshots.

**Highlights**: When it's time to end an experience or say good-bye, Captions offers the chance to reminisce, share, appreciate, and make a statement about the past. People can articulate their feelings of shared experience, the wins, the losses, the growth, the change, and the celebration. A diversity of contributions from each person broadens the plane of their understanding and enriches the whole.

**Preparation**: Gather the group into a circle.

**Script**: *This exercise is about sharing what we would like to see in a company scrapbook. Imagine an 8 x 10 photo of each of you will be displayed in this album. As we stand here, take a moment to remember and think about a favorite, most memorable, poignant, challenging, or informative time during our program that you would like to have recorded for posterity in this imaginary scrapbook.*

*Your memory can have occurred within a single day or over several days together. If we had taken a snapshot of you during that time, what would you have been doing? What will you remember most? When you have that memory in your mind, put your thumb up to let me know you are ready to continue* (wait for all thumbs to go up).

*Now, with the snapshot of this memory in your mind, think of a caption of ten words or less to illustrate your memorable picture. Make your caption expressive, so that someone hearing it would immediately know the essence or the meaning of your snapshot. Again, thumbs up when you have a caption and are ready to share* (wait until thumbs go up). *Okay, who would like to share first?*

**Variations**: Another common version of this is <u>Headlines</u>, where people report a potential newspaper headline. You could also ask for the title of a book, TV show, movie, song or video game.

# 81                                    HANDS UP!

**PROPS**: 0 (none)
**MOVE**: 1 (light / standing)
**AREA**: Medium
**TIME**: 0-5 minutes

**SIZE**: Any (individuals)
**TYPE**: Closer (O, S, F, E)
**ORIGIN**: Craig Dobkin
**REFERENCE**: New

Raise your RIGHT hand!

Lower your LEFT hand!

**Intent**: Experience and discuss leading, following and resisting.

**Action**: People raise and lower hands as they stand in a circle.

**Highlights**: When people are holding hands, any movement with one of their hands produces movement in their neighbor's other hand. Do people lead, follow, and/or resist such movements?

**Preparation**: Ask people to gather in a circle and hold hands.

**Script**: *What we're going to do next is an analogy for our group as we leave this gathering and move back out into the workday world. Some of you resist and some of you lead the way. And all of you can follow a strong leader...or be one. Ready? Raise your right hand!* People raise right hands and all the left ones go up as well.

*Now lower you left hand!* People lower left hands and all the right ones go down as well. *What happened there?* Hold a debriefing on leadership, followership, and resistance to these notions; and/or discuss who experienced any resistance to their leadership.

*Yes, let's try it again. This is a model for moving forward. Notice that sometimes you are a leader and sometimes you are a follower. Try to refrain from being a resister. Ready? Raise your right hand! Now look around and memorize this picture in your mind. When you step up and lead, others will follow. Sometimes, they can't help but follow! So, in celebration, shake your neighbor's hand and 5 more hands before you leave. Thanks for coming today.*

**Variations**: In closing activities, where a circle is holding hands, a nice beginning is to have everyone share a <u>Round</u> or take their turns in sequence to give a single word or phrase that reflects on their experience. Rounds can be about lessons learned, personal pledges for future change, observations of people, and performance scaling (asking for a show of digits, or a number from 0 to 10, on a topic).

An equally fun ending is <u>ET Closure</u>, where people simply point to themselves (with their index or ET finger) and say "GO HOME!"

# 82　WONDERFUL CIRCLE

**PROPS**: 0 (none)
**MOVE**: 1 (light / standing)
**AREA**: Medium
**TIME**: 15-30 minutes

**SIZE**: 10-20
**TYPE**: Closer (S, F, E)
**ORIGIN**: Matt Weinstein
**REFERENCE**: PF-58

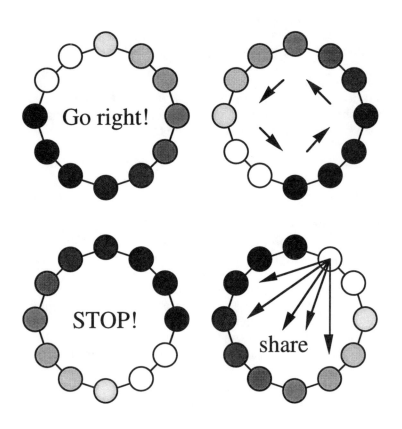

**Intent**: Speak freely and openly about aspects of an experience.

**Action**: People gather in a tight circle to share.

**Highlights**: Encourage your group to participate earnestly, as sarcasm or disrespect will ruin their closure. Wonderful Circle is sometimes slow to start, but picks up speed as people, who may deny attachment or avoid feelings at the end, begin to reminisce. Occasionally, contributions may be funny, outrageous, or even "off-color" due to 1) concern that participants will be forgotten, 2) the discomfort of saying good-bye, and/or 3) the need to move on. This activity includes a countdown designed to mark the ending.

**Preparation**: Ask people to gather in a tight circle by linking arms.

**Script**: *Before we leave, this is an opportunity for each of you to say anything you like to the group about our time together. It may be a poem, song, insight, vision, appreciation, or anything else you would like to share. Each person will have a brief opportunity to say something. Active listening is just as important as speaking.*

*In addition, we will provide a supportive place for those who don't usually speak out in groups to do so. When I say GO RIGHT the entire circle will shuffle to the right* (demonstrate). *When someone has something to share, they will call out STOP, that person will then speak and say GO LEFT once they have finished speaking. Once again, we will shuffle left, until someone else calls STOP!*

*This sequence repeats until we note a period of silence. At that point, I'll ask, ARE WE DONE? If no one speaks, we'll begin a quiet countdown from ten to zero and anyone can interrupt this with a STOP! When we reach zero, we're finished and will end with....* (describe a suitable celebration event). *Any questions? Go right!*

**Variations**: The shuffling right or left provides distraction from long pauses while people prepare to speak. If you want to focus on silence, by all means do away with the "go right, go left, and stop!"

# 83                                     LATER LETTERS

**PROPS**: 2 (two or more)          **SIZE**: Any (individuals)
**MOVE**: 0 (none / sitting)          **TYPE**: Closer (F)
**AREA**: Small                           **ORIGIN**: Classic
**TIME**: 15-30 minutes              **REFERENCE**: New

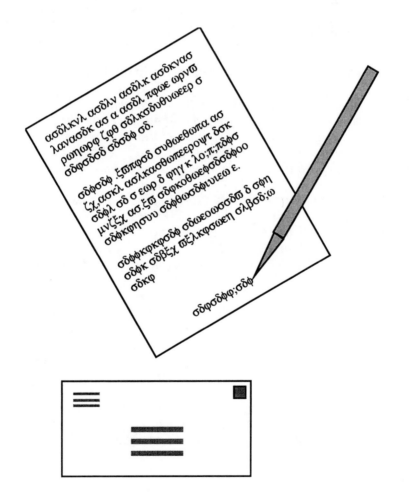

**Intent**: Capture and express reflections on personal experiences.

**Action**: People write a private letter to themselves (mailed later).

**Highlights**: People also address their envelopes to themselves and the letter is posted to them, a few months after the program is over.

**Preparation**: Distribute pens, paper, and pre-stamped envelopes to all. Ensure they have quiet space with an adequate writing surface.

**Script**: *I'd like for you to look ahead several months or more and picture yourself receiving your mail. You find the usual collection of bills, advertisements, and junk mail. Upon closer inspection you find a personal letter with familiar handwriting: YOURS! You remember back to this program closure, when you wrote yourself a personal letter and gave it to us to post on your behalf months later.*

*You open the letter and as you read your own handwriting, you are transported back to that earlier time. You wrote several things that were true for you then: 1) a few feelings about the training...what was productive and what wasn't, 2) something you were anxious to get back to work to accomplish, 3) a note about a new relationship you had created, 4) a goal you had publicly committed yourself to accomplish, 5) a description of the raucous banquet or another memorable event, and, amazingly enough, 6) a short poem, that didn't rhyme, illustrated by some doodles. You did a lot in those 20 minutes and the letter is a timely reminder of your experience.*

*Now, please take a pen, paper, and pre-stamped envelope. Write yourself that very letter. When you finish, sign it, put it inside the envelope, seal it and write your own address and return address on the front. Put it in this pile to be mailed later. The letter is yours and no one will read it except you. Write as much or as little as you are compelled to. Use the previous suggestions or make up your own. Find a quiet spot alone, which supports reflection, and cease all conversations until we are finished 20 minutes from now.*

**Variations**: You may guide the letter writing with questions about learning, change, future action, differences, barriers, and resources.

# 84                                       YARNING

**PROPS**: 2 (two or more)          **SIZE**: 10-20
**MOVE**: 1 (light / standing)       **TYPE**: Closer (O, S, F)
**AREA**: Medium                     **ORIGIN**: Classic
**TIME**: 15-30 minutes              **REFERENCE**: New

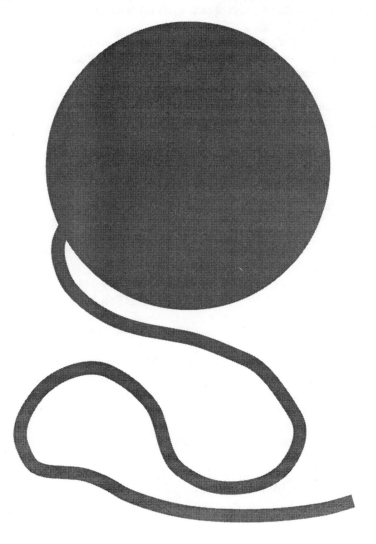

**Intent**: To connect visually through shared experiences.

**Action**: People toss and unwind a ball of yarn to create a network.

**Highlights**: The network or "web" can then be displayed.

**Preparation**: This game uses a lot of yarn. Make sure you have a BIG ball of medium to heavyweight colorful yarn and some extra in reserve. In addition, you'll need several blank adhesive labels, one colorful marker, and one thumbtack per person (or a roll of masking tape). Tack or tape mount the final web onto the wall, ceiling, or floor. Gather the group into a circle, standing shoulder to shoulder.

**Script**: *Before we begin this closing, I'd like everyone to print, on one of your sticky labels, a single word that describes how you feel about your experience today.* People take a few seconds to do this.

*Now, using the yarn, we will visually and metaphorically "tie" ourselves together according to our common experiences. For example, my word is INSPIRED! So, I attach my label to the yarn* (looks like a flag) *and roll the ball of yarn along the ground or toss it to someone across the circle. Note that I hold the end, while the ball unravels.* As you speak, clearly demonstrate these actions.

*The next person adds a label and passes the ball on, while holding their segment of the labelled yarn and continuing to unravel the ball. Once all the yarn has been used to create a networked web between us, the last person can toss or roll the ball to me and I'll tie it off. Any questions? Okay, let's start connecting....*

*Now, we can place other labels at the intersections of yarn in order to create stronger connections among us.* People attach their last words. *The final challenge is to attach our web to the ceiling, floor, or wall by using the tacks or tape, and in a way that all our words are clearly visible. Who knows how to do this? Please proceed.*

**Variations**: Double labels can be used back to back so the "web display" can be mounted between two posts and viewed from both sides. Label words can be about anything you or the group desire such as lessons learned, applications, and commitments to change.

# 85                    BALLOON BALANCE

**PROPS**: 2 (two or more)        **SIZE**: 1-10
**MOVE**: 1 (light / standing)     **TYPE**: Closer (O, S, F, E)
**AREA**: Medium                   **ORIGIN**: Karl Rohnke
**TIME**: 15-30 minutes            **REFERENCE**: New

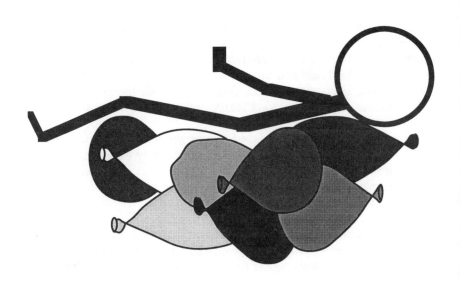

**Intent**: Identify supporting factors that help balance people.

**Action**: Group balances a member on a bed of supportive balloons.

**Highlights**: Make sure the ground or floor being used is not likely to burst balloons; or use a tarp or blanket beneath the balloons.

**Preparation**: Distribute one 11" latex balloon to each person. Ask them to inflate it and tie off the neck. Have extras ready to cover breakage. Ask people to write their names on their balloon using broad tipped permanent markers (NOT pointed pens). Consider using balloon colors to divide a large group into several small ones.

**Script**: *In addition to your name, write something on the balloon that you personally do to support people in your group as they try new things and take risks.* People do this. *Now, we need one volunteer who is willing to try something new and take the risk of being balanced on your groups' supporting balloons. Any takers?*

*Okay, the challenge is to float or balance this risk taker, who may metaphorically represent the team or your company, on a bed of support without that floater touching anyone or anything other than balloons and without anyone holding balloons in place. You may help your group member into position, but final support must be by balloons only. Any questions?* Give the group ten minutes to strategize, then five minutes to actually "support" the person. Decide in advance, if you will allow other small groups to share their unneeded balloons, to symbolize sharing company resources.

**Variations**: Extend the challenge by very carefully withdrawing one balloon at a time and experimenting with the fewest number needed to support a person. Support several people, side by side. Change the topic from support to commitments or contributions. Debrief and discuss what was written on each person's balloon.

What to do with leftover balloons? Many can be used later in the day, or you can challenge partners to hug one another, and break a balloon while squeezing it between their bodies: otherwise known as <u>Fire in the Hole</u> (see also game #40: Balloon Introductions).

# 86                    METAPHORIC TOOLS

**PROPS**: 2 (two or more)      **SIZE**: 10-20
**MOVE**: 1 (light / standing)   **TYPE**: Closer (O, S, F)
**AREA**: Medium               **ORIGIN**: Faith Evans
**TIME**: 15-30 minutes        **REFERENCE**: New

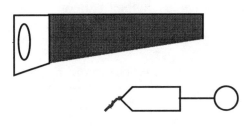

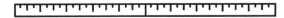

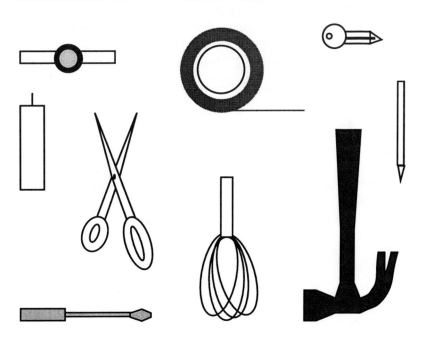

**Intent**: Describe oneself (or lessons) using tools as a metaphor.

**Action**: Folks pick tools that represent their lessons or themselves.

**Highlights**: Using actual objects to inspire metaphors works well.

**Preparation**: Secure a large collection of tools (saw, tape measure, scissors, candle, screwdriver, duct tape, egg beater, whisk, broom, key, stop watch, glue, pencil, etc.). Arrange tools randomly on the ground and gather the group in a circle around them.

**Script**: *As we close today, we'll be using the tools that you see here as metaphors that may represent your learning, our collective vision and mission, your contributions to the day, or who you are as a person* (use whatever supports the work of the program).

*Now I'd like for each one of you to wander among these tools, handle them if you want to, and mentally choose the one that best represents your experience of our time together. For instance, I might choose that Swiss Army knife* (point to the tool) *because I understand that one tool doesn't solve every problem and I want to be ready for the unexpected. Or, I might choose that magnifying glass* (point to it) *to focus on both bigger pictures and finer details.*

*When you have chosen your tool in the next five minutes, step back to our original circle. Leave your tool there in case someone else likes it just as much as you do. However, pick up the tool when it is your turn to share your interpretations and then return it when you're finished.* (After five minutes, when people have chosen their tools and returned to the circle), *who wants to share first?*

**Variations**: Instead of tools, use a collection of textbook titles or natural objects collected by the people themselves.

# 87           BLOWING BUBBLES

**PROPS**: 1 (one only)
**MOVE**: 1 (light / standing)
**AREA**: Medium
**TIME**: 5-15 minutes

**SIZE**: 20-50
**TYPE**: Closer (O, F)
**ORIGIN**: Faith Evans
**REFERENCE**: New

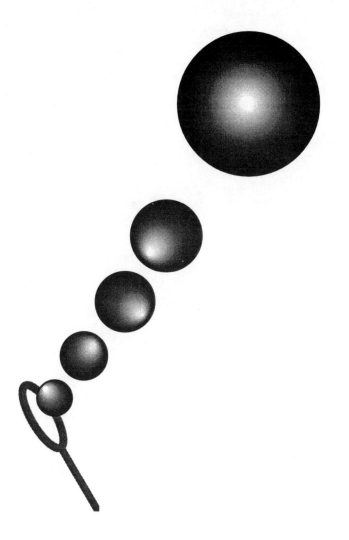

**Intent**: Finding program lessons and life metaphors in bubbles.

**Action**: People blow bubbles and discuss metaphors of the day.

**Highlights**: Blowing bubbles is especially effective for changing peoples' states of mind following heavy or difficult meetings. This playfulness allows creativity, imagination or spontaneity to surface.

**Preparation**: Give one small bottle of bubbles (with wand) to each person (order economically from Oriental Trading 800-327-9678).

**Script**: *I'd like you to take one of these bottles and do what seems natural* . Wait to see who blows bubbles first and if no one does, quietly open your bottle and begin blowing. *Spend a few minutes just playing freely with bubbles.* Allow time for people to do this.

*In these bubbles, I'd like you to find a metaphor for your program experience. What do these bubbles remind you of regarding the day, its highlights, yourself, and other people? What about their shape, color, and texture is like your work, company, and future? Okay, take a few moments to think about your own metaphor and when you are ready to share it with the group, put your thumb up.*

People share: "This solution was merely a liquid in a bottle until I held it up to the light and added my breath and energy. Only then did the liquid transform into something different and beautiful. If our vision is to transform our department, I'll need to add more of my own energy to make something different and wonderful occur."

And another: "A long and steadily calibrated breath (or work effort) results in a longer lasting bubble. Short, quick puffs make small bubbles that pop quickly."

**Variations**: Have extra bottles of bubbles for people to take home to their families or friends. Consider adding company logos to the bottles.

# 88    ANONYMOUS APPRECIATION

**PROPS**: 0 (none)                **SIZE**: 1-10
**MOVE**: 2 (moderate / walking)    **TYPE**: Closer (S, F)
**AREA**: Medium                   **ORIGIN**: Craig Dobkin
**TIME**: 5-15 minutes             **REFERENCE**: New

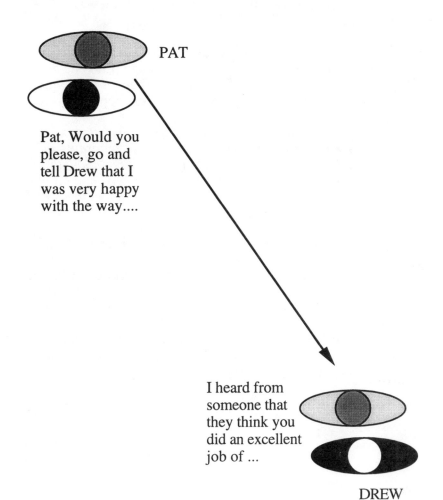

PAT

Pat, Would you
please, go and
tell Drew that I
was very happy
with the way....

I heard from
someone that
they think you
did an excellent
job of ...

DREW

**Intent**: Offer and receive appreciative feedback from colleagues.

**Action**: People send appreciation through a neutral emissary.

**Highlights**: Positive appreciation is almost as challenging to hear as negative feedback. Even when the appreciation is sincere, people can discount or neutralize it, and wonder why they are undervalued.

**Preparation**: Get people into a circle about shoulder width apart.

**Script**: *There are many ways to give and receive appreciation. One is face to face. Another is hearing comments through a grapevine. A third, more fun and mysterious way, will be part of our closing. We are going to focus on appreciating one another anonymously.*

*In a moment, you will have the opportunity to give some positive comments to someone through a third party messenger. In other words, I say to Pat, "Please tell Drew the following, and without mentioning my name!"*

*This is also an exercise in listening. Listen to the appreciation being given to you by the neutral messenger and also listen when you are the messenger to make sure you transfer the message correctly!*

*Make your appreciations, short, vivid, and specific. Single sentence messages are best. Keep appreciating as many people as you can, and remember to soak it up when someone appreciates you. Any questions? Let's reflect silently for a few minutes on what to say to each person. I'll let you know when ten minutes is up and you can begin sending your messages. Any questions?*

**Variations**: Do NOT assume this will work for negative feedback. If a group is receptive to more direct feedback, try Back Writer. In this activity, ask people to tape a sheet of paper to their backs and everyone can write positive comments on their back pages.

# 89                          GALLERY WALK

**PROPS**: 2 (two or more)
**MOVE**: 0 (none / sitting)
**AREA**: Medium
**TIME**: 30-60 minutes

**SIZE**: 20-50
**TYPE**: Closer (S, F)
**ORIGIN**: Classic
**REFERENCE**: New

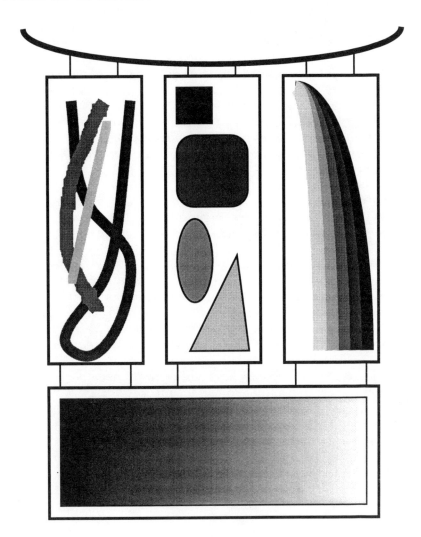

**Intent**: A picture is worth a thousand words: debrief by drawing.

**Action**: Small groups create illustrated "experience" galleries.

**Highlights**: Starting to draw is the hardest part of this one. Many people have negative childhood voices telling them they can't draw. Encourage spontaneity with whimsical tendencies and down play perfection. Authentic expression in the goal. Use groups of 4-6.

**Preparation**: Distribute supplies of chart paper, colorful markers, and masking tape (or clothespins and a clothesline to hang the art).

**Script**: *One half hour from now is the opening of a new art gallery that is extremely exclusive, highly creative and very informative. The gallery artists are you and the theme is your own experience.*

*Your small group works together to illustrate insights from the day using symbols or metaphors. Each person contributes some drawing to the final collaboration. When the gallery opens, each of you will also contribute part of the verbal group presentation of your masterpiece. Make these presentations informative, entertaining, and brief.*

*Now in case you are groaning and looking for the nearest exit, remember that your gallery art and presentation is a collaborative team effort. You might consider sports or nature for some initial inspiration. Only pictures drawn on the paper. No written words, other than the artists' signatures. You have 30 creative minutes until "Show Time!" Any questions?*

Walk around to encourage and support groups as they act jointly to define their structure for expression. Shorten the delivery timetable if necessary. In preparation for "Show Time," invite groups to tape their finished art on the wall or clothespin it to the rope. Invite groups to present their work, one at a time. Lead the applause. Encourage them to take their artwork back to the office for display.

**Variations**: If drawing is a stumbling block, try sculpting with modelling clay,collages, or finger painting. Musical composition and dramatic presentations are other alternatives.

# 90                                PERCEPTION CARDS

**PROPS**: 2 (two or more)        **SIZE**: Any (partners)
**MOVE**: 1 (light / standing)    **TYPE**: Closer (O, S, F)
**AREA**: Medium                  **ORIGIN**: Classic
**TIME**: 15-30 minutes           **REFERENCE**: New

| | | | |
|---|---|---|---|
| pleased | gratified | energetic | positive |
| depressed | protective | curious | encouraged |
| happy | enthusiastic | alive | content |
| challenged | drained | attentive | resigned |
| engaged | obstreperous | alert | frustrated |
| charged | vigilant | bored | undervalued |
| distracted | exhausted | tired | angry |
| defensive | irritated | awake | audacious |
| resentful | blue | respectful | dubious |
| annoyed | reflective | ornery | unappreciated |
| trusting | observant | guarded | bold |
| eager | aware | inspired | confident |
| satisfied | friendly | mindful | wary |
| upbeat | enlivened | hopeful | reassured |
| expectant | anticipating | mistrusting | cautious |

**Intent**: Raises awareness about people's different states of mind.

**Action**: People select pre-printed cards and dialogue with partners.

**Highlights**: Although presented here as a closer, this activity can be used at anytime during a program to check in with how people are feeling. You are the tone setting role model for this activity.

**Preparation**: Acquire approximately 100 indexed perception cards by making your own (starting from the list opposite) or ordering a set from Project Adventure (1-800-253-9784). Perception cards contain single words that express various sensitivities, emotions, feelings, moods, and reflections. Randomly scatter the cards on the ground. Have a few extra blank ones and pens for people to make their own. Ask folks to find a partner they don't know very well.

**Script**: *On the ground are about 100 cards printed with descriptive words. Tune in to yourself for a moment to ascertain your current state of mind. Then pick up 3 blank cards and a pen and circulate among these cards on the ground and write down two words that most accurately describe your mood. There are no right or wrong feelings here and you are validated for what is true for you now. If you don't find the best word, by all means, write your own down.*

*Now, stop again and check in with yourself to discover what you would prefer to be feeling now. Find those words and write them on a second blank card. Think about the results you want and the emotions you'll need to experience in order to get those results.*

*When you have written a current mood and a desired state, return to your partner and discuss the words you chose. You have about 3-5 minutes for each of you to share at a level you are comfortable with, while the other partner simply listens. I'll tell you when to switch.*

(Once both have shared), *now take five minutes each to discuss what you will do in order to achieve change in your state of mind.*

**Variations**: Ask people to pick cards that represent others in the group and place these selections inside a suitable container for each person. Use cards with descriptive pictures instead of words.

# 91                    CELEBRATION CIRCLES

**PROPS**: 0 (none)                **SIZE**: Any (small groups)
**MOVE**: 3 (heavy / moving)       **TYPE**: Closer (O, S, F, E)
**AREA**: Medium                   **ORIGIN**: Faith Evans
**TIME**: 30-60 minutes            **REFERENCE**: New

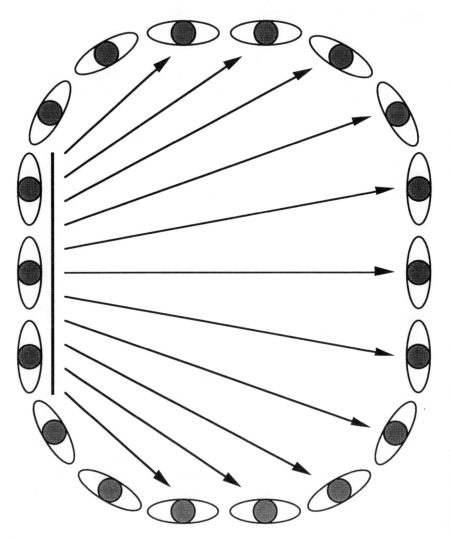

**Intent**: Celebrate valuable lessons in the program experience.

**Action**: Small teams create, teach and lead others in a celebration.

**Highlights**: Celebrating is a natural extension of an interactive day of experiential learning. Guide groups to celebrate the day's content and not its end. Celebration circles is different from group skits.

**Preparation**: To insure maximum participation, use intact groups or form small groups of 3-5 where possible. Each group spends 15 minutes designing a celebration that fits the end of the day and that can be taught in a single demonstration to the other groups. Emphasize that a theme for the celebration might be to identify and commemorate what was learned including powerful insights, humorous episodes, significant events, or valuable lessons. Highlight that the celebration should be short, vivid, specific, and inclusive (meaning everyone is able to repeat it). When the celebration groups are ready, gather everyone in a large circle.

**Script**: *Okay, we're ready for final celebrations. You know your order of presentation and each group needs to follow quickly after the previous one. This should proceed in rapid fire succession.*

*Each group will enthusiastically present your celebration for all of us to observe. Then you will immediately present it again in a way that we can learn it on the second time. Finally, we will all repeat it back to you on the third time. And then, we'll applaud the efforts and progress to the next group. Any questions? Is everybody ready? Let's have group one. Group two stand ready on deck!*

Your large group management is critical in establishing the pace and sequence of the celebrations. Keep the energy and participation high by moving quickly and intentionally from group to group until everyone is finished. Don't permit pauses to dull the excitement.

**Variations**: If the groups are celebrating well together, end this one with another round that repeats all the celebrations in sequence with one continuous grand celebration and no demos in-between. See also #27: Team Cheer.

# 92 RECOGNITION RINGS

**PROPS**: 0 (none)
**MOVE**: 0 (none / sitting)
**AREA**: Medium
**TIME**: 5-15 minutes

**SIZE**: Any (small groups)
**TYPE**: Closer (F)
**ORIGIN**: Classic
**REFERENCE**: New

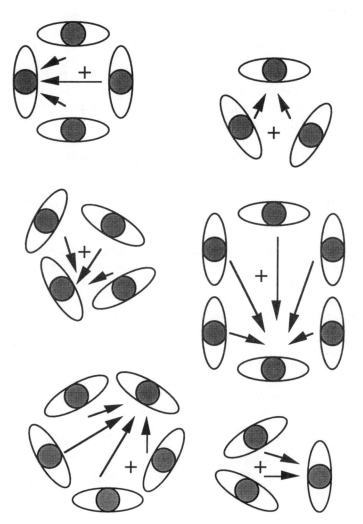

**Intent**: Recognize and appreciate colleagues.

**Action**: People give positive affirmations in small groups.

**Highlights**: Though the process may be uncomfortable or produce vulnerability for some, especially in the beginning, learning to give and receive acknowledgement is an invaluable skill worth practicing. Not everyone must share, since heartfelt authenticity is more treasured than numbers of speakers. This is reminiscent of the old "Hot Seat" activity, but minus negative feedback.

**Preparation**: Unless you have an intact group, seat people in tight circles of 3-8 and disperse these small groups far enough apart that they can't hear among groups, but can hear within their own circle.

**Script**: *Each person in every circle will have an opportunity to give and receive acknowledgement. We'll take turns being the recipient of these affirmations and silently listening to the appreciations for two minutes. The recipient may only respond with a "Thank You," then we'll celebrate and move on to the next person.*

*We'll also take turns giving positive feedback and will make it vivid and specific, so that everyone can heard in the two minutes we have available. Any questions? Okay, who wants to volunteer first?*

Keep track of the time and announce a switch to the next recipient every two minutes, after celebrating each recipient accordingly.

**Variations**: <u>Two Strokes and a Wish</u> involves providing feedback that includes two positive pieces (stroke) sandwiched around a negative (better expressed as a wish for something different). The key is a supportive and trusting environment as some people may feel uncomfortable or vulnerable.

Since stating wishes can be most challenging, frame these around what you wish the person might do differently (don't criticize) or more of (rather than less of). Try and make these positive as well. Again, both strokes and wishes should be short, vivid and specific.

# 93        BODY PART REFLECTION

**PROPS**: 2 (two or more)      **SIZE**: 10-20
**MOVE**: 1 (light / standing)    **TYPE**: Closer (F)
**AREA**: Medium                **ORIGIN**: M. Cummings
**TIME**: 15-30 minutes         **REFERENCE**: New

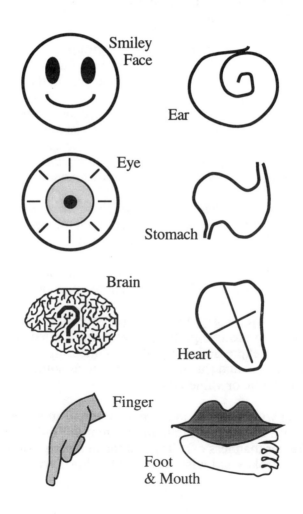

Smiley Face

Ear

Eye

Stomach

Brain

Heart

Finger

Foot & Mouth

**Intent**: Provide some interesting topics for debriefing discussions.

**Action**: People respond appropriately to thoughtfully chosen items.

**Highlights**: People pass around, or toss back and forth, one of several items (balls) that represent different types of things. The balls can be purchased at novelty shops or you can make your own.

SMILEY FACE BALL: something that made you smile OR happy.

EAR BALL: something you heard while in the group OR words that captured your attention.

EYE BALL: a vision you have for the group OR something new that you saw in yourself or in others.

STOMACH BALL: something that took guts for you to do OR something that pushed you outside your comfort zone.

BRAIN BALL: something new that you learned about yourself OR something you never thought of before this program.

HEART BALL: some new emotion you experienced OR a feeling that you had during an activity.

FINGER BALL: something that touched you OR the description of a new direction or goal you wish to proceed toward.

FOOT & MOUTH BALL: something you wish you hadn't said OR an example of where you really walked your talk.

**Preparation**: Ask folks to circle up, standing shoulder to shoulder and introduce one ball at a time (do not use multiple balls together).

**Script**: *When you catch this ball* (show what it is), *I'd like you to respond to this statement* (select one from the pairs above) *by sharing something that is true for you. Any questions?*

**Variations**: If balls are unavailable, substitute drawings on cards. Ask people to select a ball or card from the pile and compose their own suitable questions before passing the ball on to someone else.

# 94          FUNERAL FOR A FRIEND

**PROPS**: 2 (two or more)       **SIZE**: 10-20
**MOVE**: 1 (light / standing)   **TYPE**: Closer (O, F)
**AREA**: Medium                 **ORIGIN**: Simon Priest
**TIME**: 15-30 minutes          **REFERENCE**: New

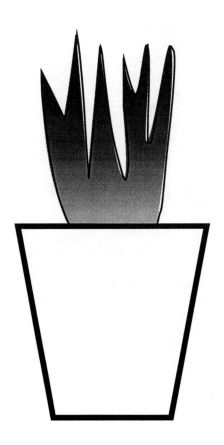

**Intent**: Bid farewell to a "bad" habit with a funeral ceremony.

**Action**: People write eulogies for their habits and "cremate" them.

**Highlights**: The ceremony here involves holding a funeral for a bad habit or "old friend." It offers people an opportunity to identify a behavior they plan on letting go of in the future and provides the chance to recruit supporters for the challenge ahead. The fact that some folks will publicly share their decisions may reinforce their ability to sustain the change after they leave the program.

**Preparation**: You'll need a fire proof metal or pottery container in which papers can be burned by a lighter or matches. Give everyone a piece of paper and a pen. Gather them into a circle.

**Script**: *As this program nears its end, each of you has identified at least one behavior that you would like to change. So we are going to have a last rights ceremony to say goodbye to those behaviors.*

*First, I would like you to name your behavior, then put your pen to paper and write a eulogy about that behavior. Please do this now.* People go away to write and return when you summon them.

*Second, we will go around the circle and place our eulogies in this container at which point they will be ceremoniously burned. If you want to read aloud prior to burning it, you may do so. In addition, if you are so inclined, you can speak about your behavior, but no one is going to insist that you talk about something that is private. If you choose to speak, I would encourage you to talk about how your friends and colleagues can support you with your recent loss. What can we do to help you "bury" your old behavior for good?*

*Any questions? Who wants to go first?* People take turns sharing eulogies, saying goodbye to old habits, and asking for support.

**Variations**: Adjust this to suit religious and personal sensibilities. You can add hymns, songs, stories, and inspirational readings.

# 95                    SOUVENIR SYMBOL

**PROPS**: 1 (one only)
**MOVE**: 0 (none / sitting)
**AREA**: Medium
**TIME**: 5-15 minutes

**SIZE**: 10-20
**TYPE**: Closer (F)
**ORIGIN**: Classic
**REFERENCE**: New

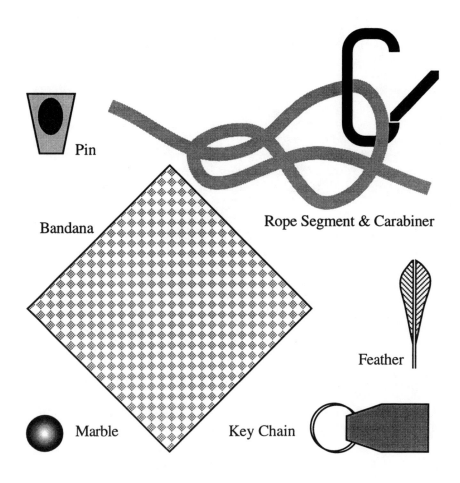

Pin

Bandana

Rope Segment & Carabiner

Feather

Marble          Key Chain

**Intent**: Create and share how souvenirs symbolize future action.

**Action**: People find, make, select and discuss symbolic souvenirs.

**Highlights**: Consider an appropriate symbol that supports future commitment to action. Souvenirs include manufactured mementos (marble, pin, key chain, carabiner, or rope segment); natural totems (pine cones, rocks, feathers, or driftwood); and memorials created from supplies (commitment bands of embroidery floss, Monkey Fist knots in rope, or images from pipe cleaners and play dough).

**Preparation**: Acquire souvenirs for people or provide materials for making them. People may keep and take these home at the end.

**Script**: *Learning doesn't occur unless behavior has been changed. Application is the key. Take some time to reflect on the changes in behavior that you have already made, or will be making soon. You may have experienced a change in attitude or in your perception of reality. You may have different intellectual understandings or emotional insights into potential change. You may want to make physical or organizational changes. Your commitment to future change may be on a personal or professional level.*

*Consider the lessons you have learned in this program and how you could apply these immediately or in the future. You may wish to use the souvenir you have in hand, as a symbol which inspires or grounds your commitment to change. Contemplate this for the next ten minutes and be prepared to share your commitment to action using your souvenir as a metaphorical springboard. Tell us what you are planning to do and by when. Ask another member of our group to support you in your efforts and tell use what you need any others to do in order to coach or support you. Any questions?*

**Variations**: Bandanas, digital certificates and instant photographs, (all embossed with your company logo) can be written upon with people's pledges and their signatures. Another option is to have people trade souvenirs or present them to others in a short ceremony (as in #78: Hidden Feedback or #88: Anonymous Appreciation).

# 96          CROSS GROUP CINQUAINS

**PROPS**: 2 (two or more)     **SIZE**: 20-50
**MOVE**: 1 (light / standing)     **TYPE**: Closer (S, F)
**AREA**: Medium                **ORIGIN**: Jan Sanborn
**TIME**: 15-30 minutes         **REFERENCE**: New

---

*Present*                          *Colleagues*
*Listening, learning*              *Working together*
*I'm clearer now*                  *We can do*
*We'll be ready tomorrow*          *What could be better?*
*Prepared.*                        *Nuthin!*


*CEO*                              *Challenged*
*Speaking, inspiring*             *New direction*
*Direction is solid*              *Hard to imagine*
*I am on board*                   *Good for us all?*
*Relieved.*                       *Try*

---

**Intent**: Meet with other groups and crossfertilize experiences.

**Action**: Group representatives gather to share learning with poems.

**Highlights**: The poetry used is Cinquain (see guidelines below), but any other form of poetry would suffice (haiku, limericks, etc.). This is a very effective way to get multiple groups sharing similar or differing insights and focus creatively on applications to their work. The resultant poems aren't as important as a cross sharing process.

**Preparation**: Individuals number off within their small groups. Gather everyone together and invite people with the same numbers (from their old groups) to form new groups. For example, all the #1's get together, all the #2's make a group, and so on. Have copies of the Cinquain guidelines available for each new group.

**Script**: *Writing poems in a group is a new activity for many of you and using the five line "Cinquain" allows everyone to succeed and work together, producing powerful and creative results.*

*The FIRST line of a Cinquain is a single word noun that sets the theme. This can be an activity you enjoyed, a feeling, a person, or something you gained: (a) learning, (b) laughter or (c) insights.*

*The SECOND line is 2 word modification of the first line using adjectives or adverbs such as: (a) extraordinary, expansive; (b) unconstrained, hearty; or (c) valuable, disquieting.*

*The THIRD line is 3 words describing action such as: (a) making tough decisions, (b) speaking our truths, or (c) learning to trust.*

*The FOURTH line is 4 words that express an emotion or ask a question, like (a) Doing the right thing?, (b) This work is challenging, or (c) Glad that I'm here!*

*The FIFTH line is another single word similar to the first line, like: (a) Exploring, (b) Accomplishing, or (c) Yeah!*

*In your new groups, take 15 minutes to dialog on how experiences in your original groups were similar and different. Voluntary scribes will be needed to record the descriptive words that are spoken. Then, take another 15 minutes to write a group Cinquain using many of the words you've recorded.*

*Let your dialog and writing focus on application to your workplace. I'll let you know when it's halftime. You have a total of 30 minutes to do both tasks. Once you've written your Cinquains, you will be invited to read them to the whole group. Any questions?*

**Variations**: Publish the resulting poems in a company newsletter. Invite people to return to their "original" groups with copies of each poem. Ask them to read all of these and then select one for reading back to everyone, thus completing the "crossfertilization" process.

# 97

# COAT OF ARMS

**PROPS**: 2 (two or more)
**MOVE**: 0 (none / sitting)
**AREA**: Small
**TIME**: 15-30 minutes

**SIZE**: Any (small groups)
**TYPE**: Closer (O, S, F)
**ORIGIN**: Classic
**REFERENCE**: QS-263

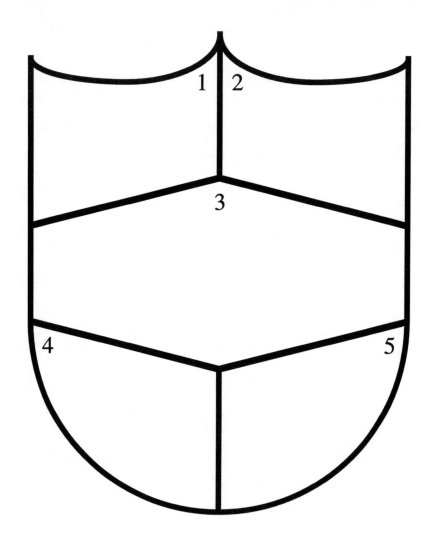

**Intent**: Aid reflection on the past, present, and/or future.

**Action**: People complete a group or personal "coat of arms" shield.

**Highlights**: This can be done as a group and/or as an individual. For collective groups, focus on reflection of past experiences and, for individuals, focus on planning for future action strategies.

**Preparation**: Distribute a copy of the shield shown, some pencils, and a variety of colored markers to the whole group or each person. For clarity, you may want to write the five items beside the shield.

**Script**: *I'd like you to represent your past experience (or future plans) in the five sections of these shields by sketching, writing, and/or drawing the following five items.*

> *GROUP:*
>
> *1. your highest level of performance in this program;*
> *2. your most enjoyable time during this program;*
> *3. a group logo that presents your best teamwork;*
> *4. the one thing your group is expert at doing; and*
> *5. something your group still needs to improve.*

*or*

> *INDIVIDUALS:*
>
> *1. your greatest personal strength;*
> *2. your most important weakness;*
> *3. a view of how others perceive you;*
> *4. a strategy or plan for bringing change; and*
> *5. the resources you need to make change happen.*

**Variations**: You can mix and match the above items, come up with your own, or ask the group members to generate a list of new ones.

# 98      TOASTING TRANSFER

**PROPS**: 2 (two or more)          **SIZE**: 10-20
**MOVE**: 2 (moderate / walking)   **TYPE**: Closer (O, S, F, E)
**AREA**: Medium                    **ORIGIN**: Simon Priest
**TIME**: 15-30 minutes             **REFERENCE**: QS-178

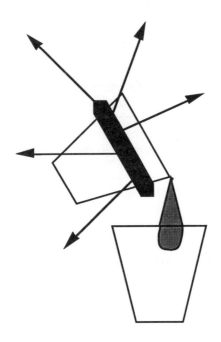

**Intent**: Share lessons and commitments from the program.

**Action**: People transfer liquid between beverage cups and buckets.

**Highlights**: This activity puts a positive spin on Toxic Waste (#57 in "101 Corporate Teambuilding Activities") by relating the liquid to what was learned and what will be different. No blindfolds needed.

**Preparation**: Provide beverage cups or insulated mugs (not made of glass) and ask people to come to the closure with water in these. Create a replica of the Toxic Waste set up. Obtain two buckets or other containers (again not glass) large enough to hold the water from all the beverage cups. Attach a tight elastic collar to one of the buckets and attach a dozen ropes to that collar with knots in the ends of the ropes. Take care that the collar or ropes do not easily detach

For indoors activities, have plastic sheets to protect against spillage If you plan on having a toast or drink to the future after the activity, be sure to clean and suitably sanitize cups and buckets beforehand.

**Script**: *As our program comes to an end, I'd like us to reflect on what we learned and what we are going to do about those lessons. Take a moment to consider your most important pieces of learning, and when you are ready, I'd like you to share those lessons as you pour your learning* (water) *into the group transfer vessel* (bucket).

(After everyone has shared and poured their water), *I'm interested in hearing what each of you is going to do in order to ensure your lessons transfer back to work. I'd like you to share your proposed change strategy, as you pick up one of these ropes at the end knot.*

(After all have shared and are holding a rope), *your challenge is to work together as a team to ensure that your learning transfers from this program* (bucket full of water) *to the office* (the empty bucket) *without spilling, and using your change strategies* (holding only the knots). Discuss the metaphors with folks after the exercise is over.

**Variations**: For an OPENER, ask folks what they bring to the day or are willing to contribute to the program, and what they expect to take away with them when they leave. For a SOCIALIZER, ask them what behavior the group can count on them to offer, and what they hope to change about themselves. Customize the questions to use this closing activity as a filler or energizer activity instead.

# 99    ALTERNATIVE REFLECTIONS

**PROPS**: 2 (two or more)
**MOVE**: 2 (moderate / walking)
**AREA**: Medium
**TIME**: 30-60 minutes

**SIZE**: Any (small groups)
**TYPE**: Closer (O, F, E)
**ORIGIN**: Unknown
**REFERENCE**: New

**Intent**: Be creative and tap into different brain hemispheres.

**Action**: People reflect on their experiences in nonverbal ways.

**Highlights**: These nonverbal alternatives to debriefing discussions are great for people who are partially new to the language used or are uncomfortable expressing themselves with words. These ways are often more beneficial or less threatening than verbal discussion.

**Preparation**: Provide plenty of (art, drama, writing, reading and other) props or supplies for those who select an alternative option.

**Script**: *Instead of reflecting on our recent program experience with words, we will be expressing ourselves differently in this closure activity. You may choose from any of the following options....*

ART: draw your feelings, paint the lessons you learned, sculpt the commitments you made in clay, sketch a cartoon of the program, graph people's energy levels during the day, or create a collage from magazine cuttings that best represents your group experience.

DRAMA: present a skit about stellar moments, reenact the highlight of your experiences, model group members into representations of your learning, or dance to interpret your most memorable emotions.

WRITING: record your lessons in journals and diaries, author a short essay about the message you obtained, express your thoughts through music and poetry, report the news regarding what really happened here, or pen an editorial on your future plan for change.

READING: tell a story about this day to a child, compare several inspirational quotes with your actual experience, make connections between the program and your life through morals, fables, legends, parables, and fantasies, or just simply scan through a new textbook.

OTHERS: photograph (pictures, slides, videotape, instant film) or map an analogy of the journey you now find yourself on as a result of today's program.

**Variations**: You can use the nonverbal alternatives above to lead into verbal debriefing discussions, if your group is so inclined.

# GAMES BY THE SIX CATEGORIES

Here is a list of all 99 games organized by the six principle types.

<u>W = WARMUPS</u> elevate heart rates or stretch muscles and joints

1 Stretching
2 Partner Stretching
3 Twisting Stretch
4 Story Stretch
5 Mrs. Grady Stretch
6 Counterbalance
7 Team Toe Touch
8 Connections
9 Rope Jousting
10 Twenty Types of Tag

<u>O = OPENERS</u> set program tone or introduce people, learn names

11 Name Roulette
12 No Props Name Toss
13 Alphabetical Name Circle
14 Name Exchange
15 Introductions
16 Let Me Introduce Myself
17 Find Your Partner
18 Crossword People
19 Give Me a Hand
20 Six Count
21 Simon Says!
22 Secret Handshake
23 Creative Greetings
24 Changing Places
25 Change Five or Ten
26 Quotes on Cards
27 Team Cheer

<u>S = SOCIALIZERS</u> collectively deinhibit people or familiarize them

28 Categories
29 Incorporations
30 Special People
31 Three Things in Common
32 Work, Rest, and Play
33 Personal Press
34 Reporters
35 Have You Ever...?
36 Wallets
37 Where in the World?
38 Dynamic Org. Chart
39 When I Grow Up...
40 Balloon Answers
41 Snail
42 Shrinking Circle
43 Welded Ankles
44 Monster!
45 Diminishing Load

F = FILLERS occupy program gaps, consume time or are sedentary

| | |
|---|---|
| 46 Seeing the Obvious | 53 Going on a Retreat |
| 47 Ping Pong Pyramid Puzzle | 54 Copy Cat |
| 48 Matchsticks & Toothpicks | 55 Mystery Writer |
| 49 Interview Questions | 56 The Virus |
| 50 Partnership Problems | 57 Acquisition |
| 51 Miscellaneous Misleading | 58 Seek & Hide |
| 52 Name of the Game | 59 Counting Shapes |

E = ENERGIZERS quickly motivate or actively enthuse people

| | |
|---|---|
| 60 Count Off! | 67 Group Charades |
| 61 Speed Animal | 68 Who is IT? |
| 62 Who Controls Who? | 69 Flashing Fingers |
| 63 Known & Unknown | 70 Gotcha! |
| 64 Foreign Exchange | 71 Circle the Circle |
| 65 The Auditor is Coming | 72 Quick Celebrations |
| 66 Stocks and Bonds | |

C = CLOSERS highlight learning, achievement and change

| | |
|---|---|
| 73 Rain Maker | 87 Blowing Bubbles |
| 74 Circle Massage | 88 Anonymous Appreciation |
| 75 Metaphoric Circles | 89 Gallery Walk |
| 76 Vortex with a Twist | 90 Perception Cards |
| 77 Dum Dum Dada Dada | 91 Celebration Circles |
| 78 Hidden Feedback | 92 Recognition Rings |
| 79 Group Photograph | 93 Body Part Reflection |
| 80 Captions | 94 Funeral for a Friend |
| 81 Hands Up! | 95 Souvenir Symbol |
| 82 Wonderful Circle | 96 Cross Group Cinquains |
| 83 Later Letters | 97 Coat of Arms |
| 84 Yarning | 98 Toasting Transfer |
| 85 Balloon Balance | 99 Alternative Reflections |
| 86 Metaphoric Tools | |

# RESOURCE GRID (Props X Time)

Use this matrix to select from the 99 activities according to how much time you have and how much equipment you want to use.

| Props by Time / PROPS | 0-5 mins. | 5-15 mins. | 15-30 mins. | 30-60 mins. | 1 hour + |
|---|---|---|---|---|---|
| 0 = none | 3, 4, 6, 8 19, 20 22, 42 69, 70 72, 73 74, 81 | 1, 2, 5, 7, 12 13, 16, 21, 23 24, 25, 30, 31 37, 38, 41, 52 53, 54, 60, 63 65, 75, 76, 77 80, 88, 92 | 10, 11, 27, 61 68, 82 | 91 | 58 |
| 1 = one only | 14, 15 51, 55 | 9, 33, 35, 36 59, 67, 87, 95 | 26, 28, 29, 43 44, 45, 47, 48 49, 57, 62, 78 | 46 50 | |
| 2 = two or more | | 17, 18, 40, 64 71 | 32, 34, 39, 66 79, 83, 84, 85 86, 90, 93, 94 96, 97, 98 | 89 99 | 56 |

1 — 10 = WARMUPS
11 — 27 = OPENERS
28 — 45 = SOCIALIZERS
46 — 59 = FILLERS
60 — 72 = ENERGIZERS
73 — 99 = CLOSERS

# CLIENT GRID (Movement X Size)

Use this matrix to select from the 99 activities according to how many people you have and how active you think they want to be.

| *Movement by Group Size*  SIZE  **MOVE** | 1-10 people | 10-20 people | 20-50 people | 50-100 people | ANY NUMBER (individuals) (partners) (small groups) |
|---|---|---|---|---|---|
| 0 = none / sitting | 32 55 | 68 95 | 18 77 89 | 49 | 26, 30, 39, 46, 47 48, 50, 53, 54, 59 83, 92, 97 |
| 1 = light / standing | 36, 51 74, 78 85 | 11, 60, 75 80, 82, 84 86, 93, 94 | 7, 42 87, 96 | 19 70 73 | 1, 2, 3, 15, 25 29, 31, 33, 37, 52 56, 69, 81, 90 |
| 2 = moderate / walking | 12, 67 72, 88 | 4, 5, 16 38, 40, 41 79, 98 | 13, 17 35, 64 76 | 28 | 8, 14, 22, 23, 34 57, 58, 63, 99 |
| 3 = heavy / moving | 9 | 27, 43, 61 | 65, 71 | 20 66 | 10, 21, 24, 62, 91 |
| 4 = extreme / lifting | | 44, 45 | | | 6 |

1 — 10 = WARMUPS
11 — 27 = OPENERS
28 — 45 = SOCIALIZERS
46 — 59 = FILLERS
60 — 72 = ENERGIZERS
73 — 99 = CLOSERS

# SELF CHECK FOR LEADING GAMES

KNOWLEDGE OF THE GAME: Do I...

[ ] ...understand the goal, guidelines and process to get results?
[ ] ...integrate the game content with the curriculum or program?
[ ] ...employ low-risk, simple group division to make subgroups?
[ ] ...have the necessary supplies and facilitative help I need?
[ ] ...have a back up activity in case this one doesn't work?
[ ] ...like the game I am leading?

UNDERSTANDING THE GROUP: Do I...

[ ] ...heed the current stage of group development for my group?
[ ] ...know that this is the right timing/placement for this activity?
[ ] ...access the group's mental, physical or emotional receptivity?
[ ] ...consider the time of day and the group's responsiveness?
[ ] ...know whether this group has done this activity before?
[ ] ...know that everyone has the ability participate fully?
[ ] ...know the adaptations/alternatives available if they don't?

DIRECTIONS: Are these...

[ ] ...short, vivid, and specific?
[ ] ...enhanced by a demonstration or written instructions?
[ ] ...inclusive of those for whom English is a second language?
[ ] ...sensitive to those who are from another culture?

VOICE: Do I use...

[ ] ...clear diction and an inviting tone?
[ ] ...examples/vocabulary appropriate to this client population?
[ ] ...naturally loud volume (or do I have a microphone/whistle)?

## EYE CONTACT: Am I...

[ ] ...direct and observant?
[ ] ...including and attending to all present?

## BODY PLACEMENT: Am I situated...

[ ] ...where everyone can see?
[ ] ...where everyone can hear?

## DEMEANOR: Am I...

[ ] ...relaxed, yet focused?
[ ] ...listening and observing?
[ ] ...humorous when appropriate?
[ ] ...confident, yet not aggressive?
[ ] ...approachable and not too cool?

## ATTITUDE: Am I...

[ ] ...safety conscious?
[ ] ...inviting and engaging?
[ ] ...gracious and nondefensive?
[ ] ...enthusiastic and authentic?
[ ] ...flexible and responsive?
[ ] ...creative and open?
[ ] ...playing and participating where appropriate?
[ ] ...having fun yet?

## FLOW: Do I...

[ ] ...change to the next game once this game has peaked?
[ ] ...leave them wanting more (too little is better than too much)?

SPACE: Is the area that I've chosen for the game...

[ ] ...large or small enough for the action and number of people?
[ ] ...appropriately indoors or outdoors?
[ ] ...full of dangers and have I dealt with these?
[ ] ...too noisy or not noisy enough?
[ ] ...sound proofed so our noise doesn't disturb others?


CLIENTS: Are they...

[ ] ...dressed appropriately for the action and location?
[ ] ...ready for this game in terms of their competence?
[ ] ...ready for this game in terms of their willingness?


WHAT IF...

[ ] ...the weather is inclement?  What's my contingency plan?
[ ] ...someone gets hurt?  Where do I go for immediate assistance?


OTHER: Add these as you discover them.


[ ] _____?

[ ] _____?

[ ] _____?

[ ] _____?

[ ] _____?

The games in this book may be used with many populations given the right modifications. The following list can be used to help stimulate your thinking about how to change the activities.

# Alex Osborn's Checklist for New Ideas *

<u>ADAPT</u>? Personalize? Change titles, metaphors, names and symbols? What other idea does this suggest? What could I duplicate? Customize to school, camp, or other settings?

<u>MODIFY</u>? New twist? Change meaning, words, goal, challenge, motion, number, sound, form, shape, size? Other changes?

<u>MAGNIFY</u>? What to add? More time? Greater Frequency? Stronger? Faster? Longer? Extra Value? Plus Ingredient? Exaggerate?

<u>MINIFY</u>? What to subtract? Smaller? Condensed? Miniature? Lower? Shorter? Lighter? Omit? Streamline? Split Up? Understate?

<u>SUBSTITUTE</u>? Who else? What else? Other ingredient? Other material? Other process? Other place? Other approach? Other tone? Other goal?

<u>REARRANGE</u>? Interchange component parts? Other pattern? Other layout? Other sequence? Transpose cause and effect? Change pace? Change schedule?

<u>REVERSE</u>? Transpose positive and negative? How about opposites? Turn it backward? Turn it upside down? Switch roles? Turn the tables? Turn the other cheek?

<u>COMBINE</u>? How about a blend? An assortment? An ensemble? Combine teams? Combine purposes? Combine appeals? Combine ideas?

* adapted from Osborn, A.F. <u>Applied Imagination</u>.
New York: Charles Scribner & Sons, 1957.

# ABOUT THE AUTHORS...

**Simon Priest** is the leading researcher and writer in experiential training and development with corporations. He presently consults in facilitation training, leadership enhancement, and executive development for a handful of progressive companies interested in staying ahead of their global competition by focusing on the development and maintenance of human resource relationships. Now early retired, Dr. Priest maintains adjunct professorships at several universities and management institutes around the world. His two most recent books are "101 of the best Corporate Team Building Activities" with Karl Rohnke and "The Essential Elements of Facilitation" with Mike Gass and Lee Gillis.

**Sam Sikes** is Vice President of Learning Unlimited Corporation. He trains facilitators and develops related indoor and outdoor training activities for adults, and has done so worldwide in a variety of corporate and educational settings. Best known for his creativity, Sam has trained groups of as few as two people and as many as three thousand. In 1996, He was recognized as regional "Practitioner of the Year" for his training achievements by the Association for Experiential Education (AEE). He also received the "Karl Rohnke Creativity Award" from AEE at their international conference in 2000, for his best-known books: "50 Ways To Use Your Noodle" (with Chris Cavert), "Feeding The Zircon Gorilla" and "Executive Marbles."

**Faith Evans** is Owner and Director of PlayFully, Inc. As a process consultant, she offers a broad range of training and development services dedicated to catalyzing life changing growth and potential in people. She specializes in experiential methodology with demonstrated strengths in action learning, small and large group facilitation and having fun! Faith is a member of both the Experiential Training and Development Consortium, and the task force that wrote the DEEP document: addressing the Definition of Experiential Education, Ethics and Exemplary Practices. Her most delightful and humbling accomplishment, however, is being continually trained by her two (now adult) offspring, Erin and Will.

# ...AND THEIR ORGANIZATIONS

The **Seventh Competence** is a collection of specialists who work with executives to develop these ten competency areas and a group of experts who focus on developing the seventh one: facilitation.

1) Valuing (ethics)
2) Thinking (systemic)
3) Communicating
4) Managing (projects)
5) Leading (processes)

6) Changing (resistance)
7) FACILITATION
8) Developing Teams
9) Developing Others
10) Developing Self

For more information please contact us by fax: 1-(253)-884-6448; e-mail: experien@tscnet.com; post: PO Box 884, Lakebay, WA, 98349, USA; or website: http://tscnet.com/~experien/.

**Learning Unlimited Corporation** (LUC) is a training company that specializes in experiential learning techniques. LUC serves a wide variety of businesses and organizations; and is recognized as a organizational leader in the industry of Training & Development using experiential methods. LUC provides facilitator training, workshops, team building, and customized programs that use cutting-edge experiential processes. For more information please contact us by phone: 1-888-622-4203; fax: (918)-622-4203; e-mail: donna@learningunlimited.com; post: 5155 East 51st, Suite 108, Tulsa, OK, 74135, USA; or website: www.learningunlimited.com.

**Playfully, Inc.** (PFI) is active in the innovation of creative course designs and dynamic breakthrough experiences for people through the field of experiential learning. Clients include a broad diversity of populations ranging from the corporate sector, through schools and colleges, to children's summer camps. PFI agrees with Plato who said, "You can learn more about a person in an hour's worth of play than a lifetime of conversation." For more information please contact us by phone: 303-702-1628; fax: 303-702-1621; e-mail: FaithEvans@aol.com; or post: 901 Reynolds Farm Lane, Longmont, CO, 80503, USA.

The authors and their organizations are members of eXperientia.

# eXperientia

is a nonprofit consulting consortium of experts in the joint fields of Experiential Learning and Adventure Programming with associates and representatives throughout the world.  The word 'experientia' comes from the Latin for "conscious learning in life derived from purposeful reflection on direct participation in action events."

FAX: 1-(253)-884-6448
E-MAIL: experien@tscnet.com
WEBSITE: http://tscnet.com/~experien/

The eXperientia Consulting Consortium
PO Box 884, Lakebay, WA, 98349, USA

## THE END

This may be the end of this book, but more importantly, it is the beginning of your own experience in personalizing and customizing what is engaging and useful to both you and your clients.

> *What we call the beginning*
> *Is often the end,*
> *And to make an end is*
> *To make a beginning*
> *The end is where we start from.*

> —*T.S. Elliot  "Little Gidding"*